DATE DUE

Treatise on Fugue

ANDRÉ GEDALGE

Treatise on Fugue

Part I:

The School Fugue

Translated by

A. Levin

Edited with an introduction by

S. B. Potter

Mattapan, Mass.
Gamut Music Company
P. O. Box 74

To the late **Ernest Guiraud**

To **J. Massenet**

the two masters without whom I could not have written this treatise

André Gedalge

Editor's Introduction

It is hardly necessary to offer justification for bringing to the English-speaking music student a translation of André Gedalge's Traité de la Fugue. This was the chief pedagogic work of a man who was revered as a teacher by a generation of French composers, and in whose classes in counterpoint and fugue sat such students as Arthur Honegger, Darius Milhaud, Maurice Ravel, and Charles Koechlin. It has been used in American universities even in its original language and has appeared in German and Italian translations. The German translation, in fact, appeared shortly after the work was written and bears the date of 1905.

Gedalge originally conceived his treatise as being in three parts, of which the part on the school fugue was to be only the first. Though the first part was the only one ever to appear, we have nevertheless thought it fitting to retain the designation Part I in the title. Gedalge died in 1926, some 25 years after completing the first volume, without bringing forth any other. This fact is itself evidence that the significance of the title bears as much on the author's concept of the scope of the subject as on his intention to write a given number of volumes. He considered the school fugue only as an opening wedge to the student's understanding of the fugue as a vehicle of musical expression in the hands of the masters. Without developing the point at length here, it is necessary only to call attention to the fact that this idea is presented in the author's own introduction and is reiterated frequently throughout the book. The school fugue itself, though its form is arbitrary, and though no single fugue can be found which exemplifies it, is still an exercise based on the common practice of composers of the 18th and 19th centuries.

The rendering into one language of ideas originally conceived in another is always fraught with dangers. It was this fact which caused the Italians to say "tradutore, traditore." Ideas are not completely independent of the medium in which they are expressed, and there is, of course, always the element of human frailty. In any case, the editor feels that it is necessary at this point to mention some specific terms which gave rise to special problems: The terms "stretto", "pedale", and "imitation" are used with broader meanings than their English counterparts. We have adopted the French connotations in order to preserve better the unity of the author's presentation. The terms are defined by the author himself in the body of the text, but we take this opportunity to point up the differences. "Stretto" is used to mean, not only the close imitation of subject and answer, but also the section of the fugue which is devoted to the presentation of these close imitations. "Pedale" means, not only a sustained tone, but also the musical material with which it is associated. The term "imitation" is the one which has the widest divergence from its English usage. It is used to mean the repetition of a melodic idea, not only in another voice, but also in the same voice. Thus, Gedalge uses an expression which means that a part imitates itself. This usage figures prominently in his discussion of the episode. In keeping with English terminology, we have found it necessary to translate the French word "coda" in two different ways: (1) as codetta when it refers to material interpolated between entries of the subject and answer and (2) as coda when it refers to material used at the conclusion of an episode.

We have felt that the rewards to be gained were worth the risks. As long as music is performed in which the fugue is a significant element of expression, the study of fugue is significant to the student. As long as the music of Bach, Beethoven, Mozart continues to appear on our concert programs, the study of fugue is significant. Its influence on composers has not disappeared in the works of the first half of the 20th century, where its adaptation to modern idioms has played an important role. In our time, the music of the Late Baroque and of Sebastian Bach has undergone a veritable renaissance. The Late Baroque was the golden age of fugue composition, and it was in the music of Bach that the fugue achieved its highest manifestation. The place of Gedalge's work in the study of fugue has long been established. We trust that enough of it has been preserved in the present version to be of value to the student.

Boston, June, 1964   S. B. Potter

Table of Contents

Modifications Which a Subject Can Undergo

In its rhythm. – In its length. – In its initial note. – In its final note. – Modifications of the answer.

Order of procedure. – Writing the answer. – Choosing the countersubjects; a new subject; strettos and canons. – Exposition. – Plan of the fugue. – Stretto. – General summary. – Over-all plan for the composition of a fugue: (1) melodic and harmonic plan; (2) plan of execution; (3) realization. – Models of complete fugues.

Preface

This treatise is divided into three parts: the first part is a detailed study of the principles governing the fugue in general and the school fugue in particular; the second part considers the different forms which the fugue may take; the third part relates the fugue to the art of musical development.[1]

I have separated the school fugue[2] from the fugue as a musical composition because I consider it not as a type of composition, but as an exercise in an arbitrary, conventional form which, in actual practice, has no application. One may argue for or against the school fugue. However, by the mere fact of its existence, the study of it has its place prepared. Wherever I could, I have tried to illustrate the rules with examples from the masters, especially J. S. Bach. I believe I am justified, in a treatise on fugue, in invoking the highest authority on the subject, namely the composer who was able to make of the fugue one of the finest and one of the most complete manifestations of the musical art. I must confess, however, that it embarasses me to have to call special attention to this fact, for it ought to be obvious that examples offered to students in the instruction of any art should be drawn from that art. Such, however, has not been the case. I therefore believe that I have made a very important innovation in music education and one which goes

---

1. Ed. note: Only the first part, which constitutes the present volume, was published.

2. I have made no distinction between the vocal fugue and the instrumental fugue because the rules are the same for both, and whatever differences there may be stem purely from the nature of voices and instruments.

directly counter to the accepted practices of tradition and school fugue style.

But even if one will admit that a school form of fugue is useful in the study of general methods, one can never protest too vehemently against the traditional practice, prevalent in various schools, of considering this form an end in itself in the study of fugue. Neither can one protest too much against a presumption that creates, with the assistance of a collection of formulas and methods, a particular style for each school: a h o m e - s t y l e as it is called in jest.

Ironically, to condemn the study of the great masters of fugue is the only point on which all theorists agree. Each one desires to set himself up as the proper authority without stopping to realize that a few judicious liberties in composition or form are not sufficient justification for casting aside the music of Bach, Handel, Mozart, or Mendelssohn. Just because Fétis, Bazin, et al think and write differently from Bach is no reason for everyone to do the same. We have the right to judge each by his own work, and we must refuse to grant these theorists the authority which they have attempted to appropriate to themselves.

Did anyone ever dream of proscribing Pascal, Bossuet, Corneille, or Molière from a treatise on rhetoric on the pretext that certain grammarians do not agree with them? And cannot one justify in music education what is done in the literary realm?

Without defining school fugue style precisely, we may point out that closely related to it is the tendency in certain circles to consider fugal composition from a point of view that is too exclusively harmonic. Because of the fact that the so-called study of harmony has been over-refined in our day, one has come to forget that, in the fugue, as with counterpoint (of which the fugue is only the highest application) chord progression comes about only as a result of the melodic flow of the parts. It is therefore obviously impossible to teach fugue on the basis of the rules of harmony, and one must not take a purely harmonic approach and hold that (for example) second inversions of major or minor seventh chords should be avoided in the fugue simply because they are second inversions. One must rather take the contrapuntal point of view and say that one cannot simultaneously sound a dissonant fourth against the third which is its resolution. The fact is that in the fugue, chords do not exist within the meaning attributed to them in treatises on harmony. We have, instead, vertical aggregations of tones which form harmony and result from the melodic movement of the parts.

It must be made clear to students that fugal composition is above all a horizontal composition. The melodic independence of the parts is limited only by the necessity of producing, at least on the first beat of each measure, a logical harmony resulting from the simultaneous sounding of the parts.[1] As a result of this liberty, simultaneous passing tones are frequently used; and harmonic analysis, such as may be applied to progressions of well-defined chords, has no possible justification here.

Nevertheless–although from the strictly contrapuntal point of view this seems to me more harmful than useful–I have consistently pointed out the passages considered at the Ecole as abuses of license. This despite the fact that I can give no reason except the one given at the Conservatory, namely, that "That is just not done." Furthermore, such observations will be useful only to those students who are preparing to take the examinations; others need not consider them.

In the study of school fugue, there are a few principles which I have been unable to illustrate with examples from the masters.[2] In these instances alone I have taken it upon myself to create them, and only because I had to. When there are so many fine models available, it does not seem at all right to say, "Me, me adsum qui feci."[3]

All the elements of this treatise were collected over a long period of teaching. They are the result of the daily contact I had with students when I took the place of my teacher, Ernest Guiraud, or when M. Massenet did me the great honor of turning over to me the direction of studies in counterpoint and fugue in his class. I always took the greatest care to note the questions which were asked and the problems which arose. In this way I became a-cutely aware of the lacunae in all the current treatises on fugue.

In order to coordinate all these various documents, I have proceeded as methodically as possible, trying to avoid every a priori affirmation, "dividing each one of the difficulties into as many small fragments as necessary to better resolve them."

1. Fugal composition is not merely polyphonic –this word has no significance here– but, more precisely "polymelodic," since the art of counterpoint consists primarily in using simultaneously, not several isolated sounds (this is the role of harmony) but several melodic parts of similar or different natures and rhythms.

2. Because the masters have never applied them.

3. I thought it was a good idea, however, to take a few examples from the fugues of my best students. Following this train of thought, it seemed to me that, since the school fugue is exclusively a student's work, I should offer to these beginners, as models, entire fugues composed by older students during the course of their studies. For I was convinced that in this way they would become more aware of the amount of skill that can be acquired at school and would try to do as well or, if possible, better by avoiding the defects of these models. (Ed. note: Several of the student fugues–those by Depecker, van Doren, Malherbe, and Morpain–have been omitted from the present edition. The others are to be found on pp. 290-326.)

By analyzing fugues of the masters and by comparing them with each other, I was able to discover their common characteristics, discarding those exceptions not common to all.

Again, "by assuming a certain order among subjects which did not appear to have any," I became convinced that all the anomalies and difficulties that the study of the fugal answer presents are removed if one recognizes the principle that theoretically the fifth degree of the main key of the subject must always be considered not as the dominant of this key but as the first degree of the dominant key. The harmonic and total consequences of this postulatum are such that the answers to the most varied subjects are in strictest accord with tradition.

This general point of view which I have consistently maintained has allowed me to develop on a broad scale certain other parts of this treatise as well and reduce to a common denominator many cases, up to now considered exceptional, that formed separate categories and were a source of great perplexity to students.

A source of great difficulty for them is the construction of the episode. From long experience I have assured myself that if the method that I have outlined is followed, these difficulties can readily be resolved.[1]

Some explanations may seem a little long. This is unquestionably due to the difficulty of the subject and to the problems I have encountered in trying to explain abstractions clearly and at the same time avoid repeating words and expressions. In any case I have tried to be as brief as possible.

I sincerely hope that from this treatise one will definitely get the impression that fugue is not, as some believe, the art of putting together a combination of sounds that are more or less musical; nor, as others believe, that it is a pretext for rehashing a few formulas that are so dearly cherished by those who did not invent them in the first place but who cling to them all the more because they comprise their sole artistic baggage. I hope that the reader will be strongly persuaded that even the school fugue is a powerful means by which to express ideas and feelings musically in a language as rich as it is varied. I hope he will also be thoroughly convinced that, even, and especially at the student level, one must find the best examples of this language, not among pedants past and present, but among the masters. I hope the study of fugue will now be freed of the harmonic subtleties which have fettered it more and more each day. Remember that har-

---

1. It goes without saying that the various methods which I analyze in the course of this treatise are not inviolable. They are merely indications to guide the student in his first study of fugue and to give him a preliminary method of work.

monic composition is pure convention and that its use is forcibly limited by a number of circumscribed combinations, always the same, while the composition of fugue and counterpoint is the only thing compatible with harmonic or melodic invention and progress in Art. Finally I hope that a little method, order, and logic will be brought into the crude empiricism of fugal instruction.

In writing this book, I have tried to illustrate that these things are possible and necessary. I should like to request that, in judging this work, one consider it not only in its detail but in its entirety. I have striven to create a work that will be useful to the Art of Music. I hope that events will prove that I have been successful. In any case, I hope it will be granted that "I have not culled my principles from my prejudices, but from the nature of things."

ANDRÉ   GEDALGE

TREATISE ON FUGUE

PART I

THE SCHOOL FUGUE

CHAPTER I

General Definitions

1. The fugue is a musical composition based upon a theme, in accordance with rules of regular, periodic imitation.

2. The name fugue (from the Latin fuga: a fleeing, flight) comes from the exclusively imitative nature of this type of composition in which the theme seems to be in constant flight from voice to voice, each part picking it up when the preceding one has finished with it.

3. To compose a fugue, it is not enough merely to imitate a theme in all the parts of a chorus or orchestra. One must also observe certain rules of modulation and texture; make use of all the devices of simple and invertible counterpoint to accompany the main theme; and present it in various aspects (imitation in direct motion, inversion, and retrograde; augmentation and diminution; canon, etc.).

4. The theme of a fugue is called the subject.

5. The imitation of the subject is called the answer.

6. A fugue may be written:
    for voices alone: this is the vocal fugue;
    for various instruments, solo or ensemble (piano, organ, violin,

string quartet, orchestra): this is the instrumental fugue;
for voices and instruments: this is the mixed fugue or accompanied
fugue.

7. The character of a fugue may vary according to the nature of the subject selected or the medium of expression (vocal or instrumental) chosen by
the composer. Whatever its nature, however, the fugal style is determined
by the consistent use of imitation.

8. The essential parts of the school fugue are:
   1. The subject
   2. The answer
   3. One or more countersubjects
   4. The exposition
   5. The counter-exposition[1]
   6. The episodes that function as transitions to the various tonalities
      in which the subject and answer appear
   7. The stretto
   8. The pedal

Each one of these points will be taken up in due course.

---

1. The use of a counter exposition is optional. It is used only in certain cases which will
be pointed out and studied later.

CHAPTER II

The Subject

9. Not every musical theme or melodic phrase is equally suitable to serve as the subject of a fugue.[1]

10. The subject of a fugue is narrowly restricted by certain necessary conditions of:

> rhythm
> melody
> length
> mode
> tonality

11. The subject should not have a large number of rhythms too different or too dissimilar from each other; two or three are enough. They should be of the same type, and one should carefully avoid in the school fugue - the only one we are concerned with here - subjects which alternate between binary and ternary meter.

Rhythm of the Subject

12. The melody of the subject of a vocal fugue should not exceed the range of a minor seventh; it is even desirable that it keep within the interval of a sixth so that the answer may lie well within the range of the voices.

In an instrumental fugue one is limited only by the tessitura of the instruments used.

Melody of the Subject

13. A subject should lend itself to various imitative combinations and to at least one canon between subject and answer, a two-part canon which provides a complete and invertible harmony - that is, with the subject providing a good bass to the answer, and vice versa.

14. The melody of a subject should always be capable of being harmonized in a natural way in four parts. If it is used in the bass, it should be able to furnish a good bass for this harmony.

---

1. The subject of a fugue should form a melodic phrase whose musical sense is complete and well-defined. It should not be interrupted by pauses on the dominant such as occur in most melodic phrases.

Length of the
Subject

15. As to the length of a subject, it is difficult to specify an average. You will later see that a small number of notes with one or two rhythms is more than enough on which to compose a fugue that is varied in its unity if one has learned well how to utilize all the resources of contrapuntal combination.

16. A subject that is too long has the following disadvantages:
   a. Since the entries are spaced too far apart, the imitative character of the fugue is considerably weakened (if it does not disappear altogether).
   b. The same notes or the same figures are repeated, hence redundancy and monotony.
   c. If the subject is not repetitious, it will have a too large variety of melodic and rhythmic elements, which will weaken the unity of the fugue.

17. On the other hand, with a subject that is too short the entries are too close together and the modulations too sudden. As a result there is a weakening or loss of tonal center.

Modality of
the Subject

18. A subject should belong completely and exclusively to one of the two modes, major or minor. One should therefore completely reject any subject which alternates between the two modes.

Tonality of
the Subject

19. A subject should be tonal, that is:
   1. It should lie wholly within a single tonality;
   2. or, if it modulates, it should include only the two keys with the closest relationship (the keys of the first and fifth degrees of the scale).
In other words, to set up a rule:
A subject can modulate only from the tonic to the dominant key, and, conversely, from the dominant key to the tonic.
Consequently, any alterations other than the ones which are involved in the modulations from the tonic to the dominant and vice versa should theoretically be considered as chromatic, that is, in no way affecting the basic tonality of the subject. This principle is of the utmost importance in the tonal relationships between the subject and the answer; but it is of value only from the viewpoint of these relationships because, beyond them, the subject can be considered as modulating to other degrees than to the fifth if the accidentals used imply these modulations, fleeting though they may be. The subject, for the most part should be in the main key.

20. A subject may begin in the main key and go to the dominant key, or it may begin in the dominant key and come back to the main key, or else it

may begin and end in the dominant key. In each of these cases, however, it should be for the most part in the main key and must use tonal chords of that key.

21. The rhythmic or melodic figure which begins the subject is called the **h e a d** of the subject.

It should have a rather well-defined character from the viewpoint of rhythm, melody, or expression.

This figure may be used two or three times in succession without interruption. Such repetition gives certain subjects an especially energetic or expressive character. (Cf. below, **Ex.** 7, 8, 9.)

The melodic or rhythmic figure used for the head of the subject should, however, never appear in the middle or at the end of the subject.

Examples:

CHAPTER III

The Answer

22. After the subject has been completely presented in one of the parts, another part imitates it.

This imitation is called the a n s w e r .

Tonality of the Answer

23. The interval at which this imitation occurs cannot be selected arbitrarily because, by definition, the answer must be followed immediately by a new entry of the subject in the main key.

24. Therefore, it is necessary for the answer to obey the same rules of modulation as the subject; that is, if there is modulation, it must remain within the limits of the two keys with the closest relationship (the first and fifth degrees of the key of the subject).

Modulation of the Answer

25. If, however, the order of modulations were the same in the answer as in the subject, the imitation would be at the unison or at the octave. This would be monotonous.

26. Therefore, the accepted practice, with respect to the answer, is to invert the order of modulations set up for the subject. Also:

1) As long as the subject remains in the key of the first degree, or main (tonic) key, the answer imitates it in the dominant key, that is at the fifth above, or by inversion, at the fourth below;

and inversely:

2) Whenever the subject modulates to the key of the fifth degree, the answer imitates it in the main key (tonic, first degree) of the subject, that is at the fourth above, or by inversion, at the fifth below.

27. Therefore it can be seen that:

When the subject does not modulate, and its tonic is the first degree of the main key, the tonic of the answer is the fifth degree of the main key;

And conversely:

When the subject does modulate and its tonic is the fifth degree of the main key, the answer, modulating correspondingly, has for its tonic the first degree of the main key.

Hence the following two rules, which apply to all fugue subjects without exception:

28. **Rule I.** Each note, altered or unaltered, belonging in the subject to the tonic key of the fugue, should be reproduced in the answer by the note, altered or unaltered, on the corresponding degree of the dominant key of the fugue (this key considered as the tonic of the answer). **Rules Governing the Answer**

In this case, the answer imitates the subject step by step, alteration by alteration, at the fifth above or the fourth below.

29. **Rule II.** Each note, altered or unaltered, belonging in the subject to the dominant key of the fugue (this key becoming, by modulation, the tonic of the subject) must be answered by the corresponding step, altered or unaltered, of the tonic key of the fugue (this key becoming the tonic of the answer as long as the subject has the dominant key as its tonic).

In this case, the answer imitates the subject step by step, alteration by alteration, at the fourth above or the fifth below.

30. The following principle is the immediate consequence of the two rules above: **Harmonization of the Answer**

The harmonies of a given fragment of the answer in the dominant key should be the same as the harmonies underlying the corresponding fragment of the subject in the main key, and vice versa.[1]

31. It is obvious that the purpose of these rules is to keep the fugue within the general tonality of its tonic key.

If the answer were always the literal imitation of the subject at the fifth above, this is what would happen: When the subject modulates to the dominant, the answer would modulate to the dominant of the dominant, that is, to the second degree of the main key. Such modulation is inadmissable because of the distance between the keys of the first and second degrees of a scale and the difficulty, under these conditions, of bringing the subject back in the main key as soon as the answer is finished.

32. Whenever the subject does not modulate, the fugue is called a real fugue, and its answer is called a real answer. **Real Fugue**

1. See Sections 39, 70 ff.

Tonal Fugue   Whenever the subject modulates to the dominant, the fugue is known as
a tonal fugue and the answer, a tonal answer.

Modulation by   33. In general, it may be recalled that one may modulate from any key
Characteris-   to its dominant key:
tic Altera-
tions

1) In the major mode, by raising (by means of a sharp or a natural can-
celing a flat) the fourth degree of the main key which then becomes the seventh degree of the dominant key.

2) in the minor mode:
    a. By raising (sharp or natural canceling a flat) the fourth and sixth
       degrees of the main key which become respectively the seventh
       and second degrees of the dominant key.

    b. By lowering (with a flat or a natural canceling a sharp) the sev-
       enth degree of the main key which becomes the third degree of the
       dominant key.

One may therefore state as a principle that any subject which has or
implies in its harmony one or the other of these alterations modulates to
the dominant key.

It must be noted carefully, however, that the aforesaid alterations may
be simply chromatic and may not affect the tonality of the subject. A careful harmonic analysis of the subject is essential to avoid such errors   and
a resulting false answer.

Modulations   34. The preceding rule applies to every type of musical phrase, whether
Peculiar to   or not it is to be used as the subject of a fugue, but it is not the only one
the Fugue   which must be applied to the modulation of a subject.

There are other conditions, applicable only to the fugue, whose purpose
is to restrict the answer to closer tonal relationship with the subject, and
which deal exclusively with the beginning, or head, of the subject and its ending.
One may state these conditions in the form of the following four rules
which will allow one to assign precisely to each tone of these parts of the
subject the degree which it occupies, either in the main key or in the dominant key. These rules are the corollary of the principle set forth above:
the harmonies of a given fragment of the answer in the dominant key should
be the same as the harmonies underlying the corresponding fragment of the
subject in the main key, and vice versa.

35. Rule I. The first degree of the main key of the subject is always considered as the root of the tonic triad:

Harmonic
Function of
the First
Degree

    1. Whenever it is used as the first or last note of the subject.

Example:

Steps of the scale of **E** maj.

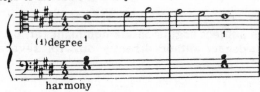

    2. Whenever the head of the subject starts on the dominant or the mediant and goes to the first degree either directly or with several notes of the scale in between. (The same rule applies to subjects which begin on other degrees of the scale, but such subjects are rare and are not found in the school fugue):

Example:

Steps of the scale of **G**

36. Rule II. The mediant (the third degree of the main key of the subject) is always considered both harmonically and tonally as the third of the tonic triad:

Harmonic
Function of
the Third
Degree

    1. Whenever it is used as the first or the last note of the subject;

---

1. The Arabic numerals placed under the staves designate the steps of the scale.

Example:

2. Whenever the subject begins on the dominant (or on any other degree) and goes to the third degree either directly or with several scale tones in between:

Example:

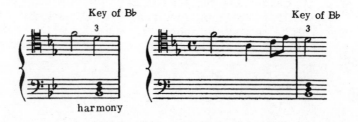

37. Rule III. The dominant of the main key is always considered as the first degree of the dominant key (root of the tonic triad of the dominant key):
   1. Whenever it is used as the first or last note of the subject;

Example:

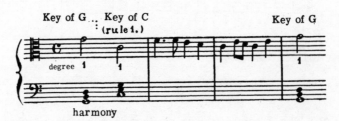

Consequently: Every subject beginning with, or ending on the dominant is considered as modulating a priori to the dominant key.

2. Whenever the head of the subject begins on the tonic, the mediant (or on any other degree except the fifth) and goes to the fifth degree, either directly or with several scale tones in between.

Example:

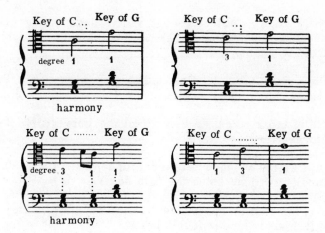

Consequently: **Every** subject going, at its beginning, from the tonic or from the mediant to the fifth degree is considered as modulating a priori to the dominant key.

38. **Rule IV.** The seventh degree of the main key of the subject (unaltered in the minor mode)[1] is always considered as the third of the tonic triad of the dominant key (that is, as the third degree of this latter key):

Harmonic
Function of
the Seventh
Degree

1. Whenever the head of the subject goes from the tonic or from the dominant to the fifth degree with the seventh degree (unaltered in the minor mode) in between.

Example:

2. Whenever the subject ends on the seventh degree of the main key (unaltered in the minor mode).

Example:

1. Note that in the modern minor scale the seventh degree is a chromatically altered step.

Consequently: **Every** subject ending on the seventh degree of the main key is considered as modulating to the dominant key and ending on the third of the tonic triad of the dominant key.

(In the minor mode the raised seventh degree always has the function of a leading tone and cannot end a subject.)

The results of these rules, as they affect the answer, will be brought out in the following sections:

Subject not Modulating: Real Answer

39. A subject does not modulate (real fugue) when it begins and ends on the tonic or mediant without using the fifth degree.

In this case, the answer reproduces it step by step in the dominant key, that is, at the fifth above or the fourth below.

Example:

40. A subject does not modulate (real fugue) when it begins and ends on the tonic or mediant and does not go immediately to the dominant (or to the seventh degree followed by the dominant) but uses the dominant either as a passing tone or an auxiliary tone, or in a sequence.

---

1. The Roman numerals under the staves designate the roots of the harmonies of the subject and answer.

Example:

Key of A minor (Tonic Key)

By eliminating the passing tones from this subject, one can see that its musical sense is the following:

and that in the first bar, the fifth degree is used only as a passing tone; in the second bar and on the first beat of the fourth bar, it is part of a sequence; finally, on the last beat of the fourth bar, it is once more a passing tone.

Therefore, one should have a real answer:

41. The same will hold for each of the following subjects:

3

Subject Beginning on the Fifth Degree. Tonal Answer

42. Any subject beginning on the dominant is considered as modulating to the dominant key.

The dominant in this case is taken as the tonic of the dominant key of the subject (Sec. 37).

It must be answered by the first degree of the main key.

Example:

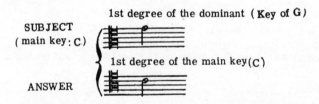

Return to the Main Key.

43. However, to be tonal, the subject must belong for the most part to the tonality of its first degree. Therefore, it must return to this tonality by using the main degrees of that scale.

Consequently:

Once the dominant is used as the first note of the subject and is considered as the tonic of the key of the fifth degree, all the notes that follow should be considered as degrees of the main key, unless they are affected by alterations characteristic of the dominant key, or unless such alterations are implied in the harmony.

Thus these other notes will be answered by the corresponding degrees of the dominant key.

Example:

44. If, on the other hand, these degrees are affected by an alteration (written or implied) characteristic of the dominant key, they will be answered by corresponding degrees of the main key.

Example:

It is obvious that the natural placed before the C (first note of the second bar of the subject) is a chromatic accidental and does not affect the tonality of D-major, on which the subject begins. The tonality of D-major is confirmed: by the sharp placed before the C on two occasions; by the harmonic sense of the first fragment; and especially by its melodic sense, which may be reduced to something like the following:

a form which necessarily calls for the following answer:

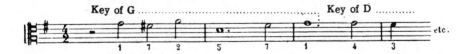

From this example it can be seen how carefully the subject must be analyzed if one wishes to distinguish chromatic alterations from tonal alterations.

45. **Exception:** Whenever a subject begins on the fifth degree followed by the raised fourth degree returning immediately to the fifth, this raised fourth degree is always considered as the leading tone of the dominant key.

Therefore, it is always answered by the leading tone of the main key, immediately preceded and followed by its first degree.

Harmonic Function of the Raised Fourth degree, at the Beginning of the Subject

Example:

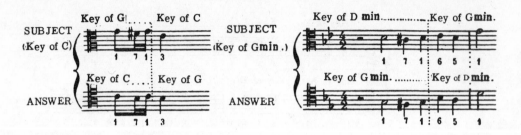

46. Except for this case, in which the raised fourth degree forms something of an auxiliary tone to the dominant, this degree always has the function of a raised fourth degree of the main key.

Example:

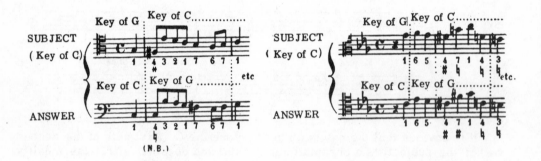

N.B. According to the rule, the fourth degree of the dominant should have the same alteration in the answer as the fourth degree of the main key has in the subject.

In this case, however, if one were to answer this alteration with the corresponding alteration, the answer would imitate the subject by inversion at that point. Answering by inversion is forbidden; it is enough to have to answer by oblique motion.

Answer to a Chromatic Subject.

47. The above anomaly comes about whenever the subject begins on the dominant and goes immediately toward the mediant or the tonic by descending chromatic motion.

The reason can be easily understood: The first degree of the main key has the same position in the scale of the dominant as the fourth degree of the dominant key. As a result, one is obliged to repeat this fourth degree in the answer until there is a real imitation of the fourth degree of the main key:

Example:

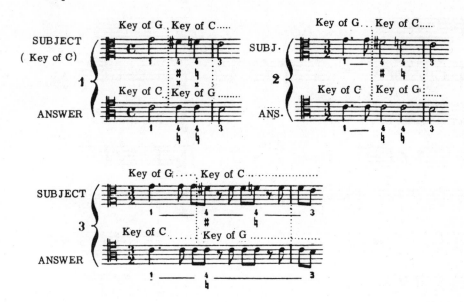

48. From these examples it can be seen how much the theme becomes distorted whenever this type of subject is given a tonal answer. Consequently, it is usually better to have a real answer to any chromatic subject going immediately from the dominant toward the mediant or the first degree.

It is different, however, when the subject goes to another degree before using the raised fourth degree. In this latter case, the answer obeys the general rule   (cf. Sec. 92 ff.: Observations on Chromatic Subjects).

Example:

49. Following are two illustrations that sum up the various aspects of the problem of a subject which goes from the dominant to the first degree, with the corresponding answers in the second column.

I. Head of the Subject Going from the Dominant to the First Degree by Descending Motion

II. Head of a Subject Going from the Dominant to the First Degree by Ascending Motion

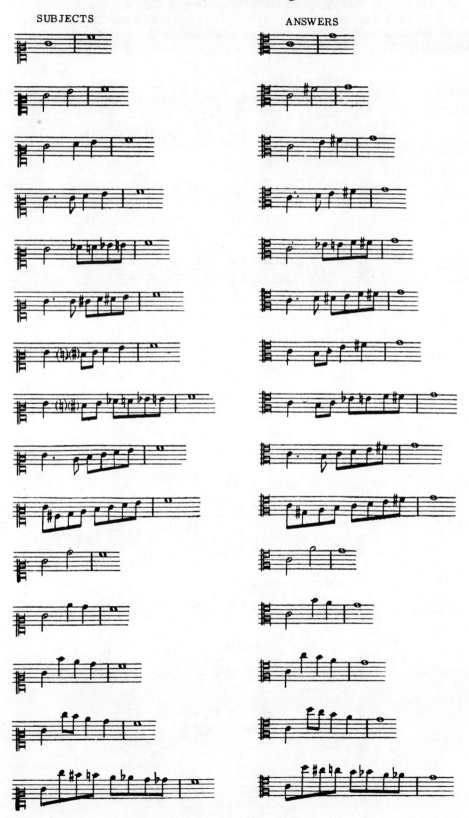

SUBJECTS

ANSWERS

50. Subjects of this type can all be illustrated by the example below which shows how each diatonic or chromatic step is affected when the subject begins on the dominant and uses various notes before going to the tonic or to the mediant.

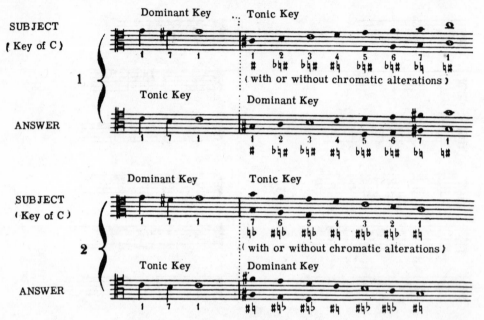

51. Practical Application of the Preceding Tables to the Heads of Subjects Going from the Dominant to the Key of the First Degree

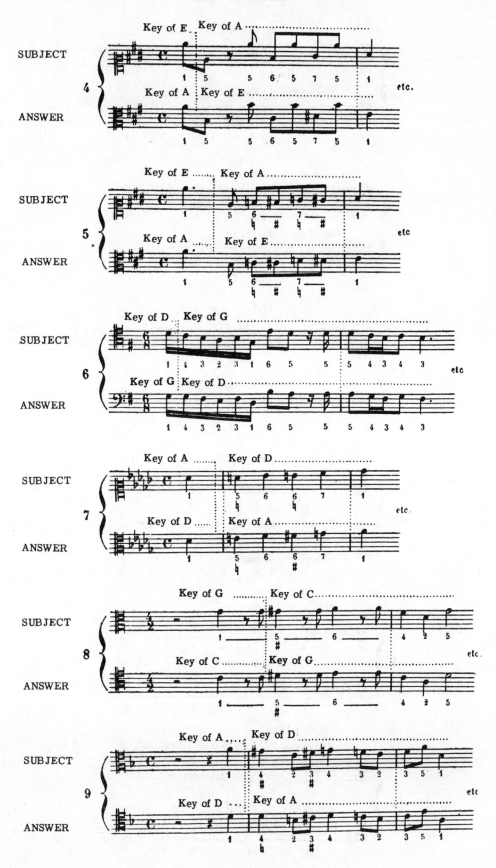

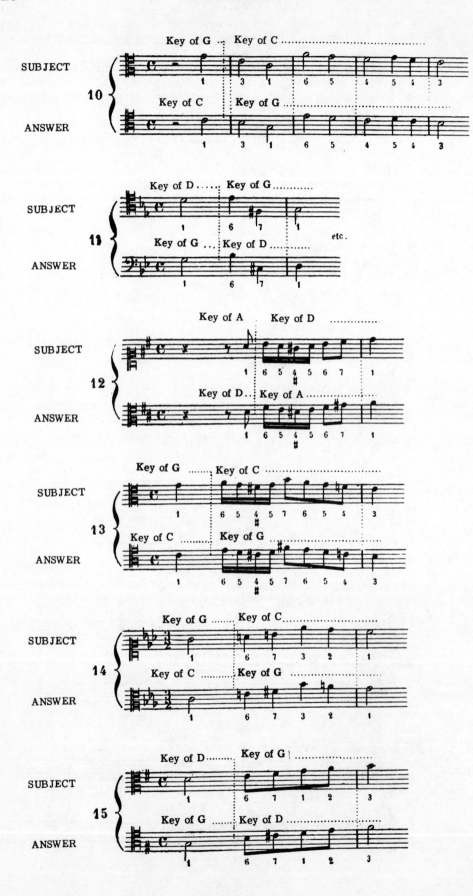

52. We have just seen that a subject beginning on the fifth degree of the main key really begins on the first degree of the dominant key to return to the main key afterwards.

The fifth degree of the main key takes on the character of the first degree of the dominant key whenever it is in the head (first melodic movement) of the subject. From this it follows that any subject which goes immediately to the dominant (or seventh degree) of the main key modulates to the dominant key and thus goes to its first (or third) degree.

This is the same as saying that, harmonically, such a subject cadences in the dominant.

53. When the first melodic movement of a subject begins on the tonic or the mediant and goes to the dominant key, one of the following situations presents itself:

The subject goes from the tonic or the mediant to the dominant of the main key:

1. directly

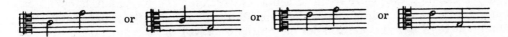

2. using the mediant immediately before the dominant whether the mediant follows the tonic without interruption,

or whether other degrees of the main key (except the fifth degree) are used in an arbitrary order between the tonic and the mediant, with the latter immediately preceding the dominant,

3. beginning on the mediant followed by the tonic immediately or with other degrees (except the fifth degree) of the main key in between, with the tonic immediately preceding the dominant in each case,

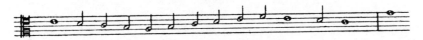

with these various degrees occurring in an arbitrary order in the subject;

4. beginning on the tonic or the mediant and using any degrees of the scale before the dominant, provided that the last note before the dominant is neither the tonic nor the mediant.

or

54. In the first three cases, all the notes preceding the dominant belong harmonically to the key of the first degree. (This does not have to be proved.)

In the fourth case, once the tonic or mediant is used as the first note of the subject, all the other notes may constitute degrees of the dominant key.

55. Here are the theoretical reasons that justify the assignment of these various degrees to one key or the other.

A modulation always presupposes a cadence. This cadence consists either of chords of the fourth and fifth degrees in succession, or of one of these two chords, or of chords of the second and fifth degrees in succession (in root position or in some inversion) going to the tonic chord of the key to which one is modulating.

If one is modulating from the first degree of a scale to the key of its dominant, this first degree ceases to belong to the main key in order to become, at a given moment, the fourth degree of the dominant key. If the modulation is made with the immediate succession of these two degrees, the pivot between the two keys occurs on one note which belongs half to each tonality, and the cadence takes the form of a plagal cadence. This is what happens in the first three preceding cases, in which the note immediately preceding the dominant is either the tonic (root of the tonic chord) or the mediant (third of the tonic chord). In constructing the answer, one cannot attribute to the tonic chord the role of first degree of the main key and fourth degree of the dominant key at the same time.

Thus, the tonic chord is always considered the first degree of the main key and the mediant, always the third of the tonic chord.

56. It is different if other degrees of the scale are interposed between the tonic (or mediant) and the dominant. The latter, as the first degree of the dominant key, will inevitably carry into this tonality every note which separates it from the initial note of the subject. All the harmonies attributed to these notes must necessarily be part of the cadence in the dominant key. This much one may be certain of, in any examples whatsoever, when determining the roots of degrees coming between the initial note of the subject and the dominant.[1] Example:

SUBJECT

ROOTS OF THE HARMONIES

I   IV   I   V   I

Key of C : Key of G

57. Here again, the pivot comes on the mediant (second note of the subject), since it alone, as third of the tonic chord of the main key and subdominant chord of the dominant key, belongs to the two tonalities which have as tonics the first and fifth degrees of the key of C, respectively. However, since the tonal attraction is stronger toward the new key than toward the key just used, and since this mediant cannot be divided between the two keys, one can only consider it as the sixth degree of the dominant key and the third of the subdominant chord of this key.

58. If, as the subject goes from the tonic to the dominant, it uses other

---

1. The dominant function attributed to these notes becomes evident if, in the examples (Sections 56 and 58) one leaves out the first note of the subject. The absolute necessity of the cadence in the key of G then becomes obvious.

degrees than the mediant, the pivot will be, as in the first three cases, on the tonic, because the latter cannot lose its function as first degree of the main key. But the other degrees, harmonically and tonally, can belong only to the dominant key.

Example:

SUBJECT

ROOTS OF THE HARMONIES

59. Applying the preceding theory, we may say that:

A subject modulates to the dominant key when it begins on the tonic or mediant and goes directly to the dominant or to the seventh degree (unaltered in the minor mode) followed by the fifth degree.

In this case the fifth degree of the main key is considered as the first degree of the dominant key and it is answered by the first degree of the main key: likewise, the tonic is answered by the first degree of the dominant key and the mediant by the third degree of the dominant key (Sections 35, 36, 37).

Head of the Subject going to the Fifth Degree (or to the Seventh Degree followed by the Fifth). Tonal Answer.

Examples:

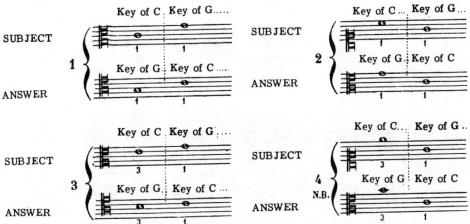

N.B. Avoid beginning a subject with this leap because of the unvocal interval resulting in the answer.

60. When the subject begins on the tonic or mediant and goes to the seventh degree (unaltered in the minor mode) followed by the fifth, this seventh degree is still considered, harmonically and tonally, as the third of the tonic triad of the dominant key (Sec. 38).

It is answered by the third degree of the main key followed by the tonic.

Examples:

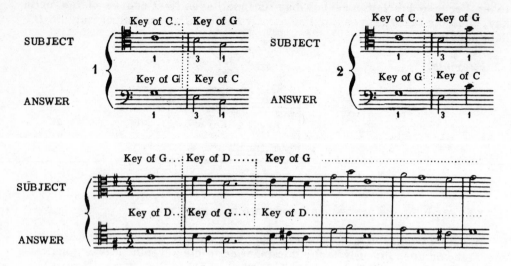

61. In such a case, in the minor mode, the raised seventh degree always keeps its character as the leading tone.[1]

It is answered by the raised seventh degree of the dominant key.

Examples:

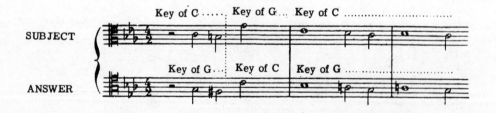

Head of the Subject. Tonal Functions of the Various Degrees

62. A subject modulates to the dominant key when it begins on the tonic or the mediant, and goes to the dominant or to the seventh degree (unaltered in the minor mode) followed by the dominant, with various other degrees in between.

All these degrees should be considered as belonging to the main key of

---

1. Because the third of the dominant key is minor.

the subject if the note immediately preceding the dominant (or the seventh degree followed by the fifth) is the mediant or the tonic.

They are answered by the corresponding degrees of the dominant key.

Examples:

63. In all the other cases, once the tonic (or mediant) is used as the first note of the subject, one must assign to the dominant key all the notes that comprise the first melodic movement carrying the subject to the dominant

or to the seventh degree followed by the dominant (seventh degree unaltered in the minor mode).

They are answered by the corresponding steps of the main key of the subject.

The unaltered fourth degree is no exception to the rule. It is always considered in this case as the seventh degree of the dominant key, and it is answered by the seventh degree of the main key.

(x the 4th degree of the main key, though unaltered, is treated as the leading tone of the dominant.)

64. It is also the same for the seventh degree of the main key (whether altered or not in the minor mode) when it is used in the first melodic movement as an auxiliary tone or as a passing tone. It is still considered as the third degree of the dominant key.

Example:

Furthermore, in the minor mode, the alterations required by the modern minor scale must be kept in mind.

Example:

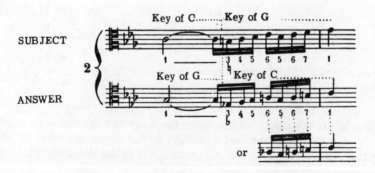

65. This rule explains an alleged false answer in a fugue of J. S. Bach (Well-Tempered Clavier, I, Fugue No. 18). In answering this subject:

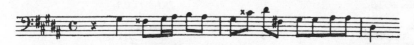

Bach considers it correctly as modulating, from the second note on, to the key of the fifth degree since the last note before the dominant is neither the tonic nor the mediant, and thus the notes interposed between the G-sharp of the second beat of the first bar and the D-sharp of the second beat of the second bar belong harmonically to the cadence in D-sharp minor. The double-sharp before the F (second note of the subject) is obviously only an accidental. Bach treats the subject as if it were as follows:

which would have as an answer:

and, by analogy he answers it like this:

and not as certain theorists would like him to:

an answer that would have no meaning either musically or harmonically. An even better idea of Bach's answer can be obtained by substituting for the F-double-sharp an F-sharp which has B for its answer or by transposing the subject to the major mode.

66. The following answers can be explained in the same way.

67. Here is a table giving various subject beginnings that go from the tonic to the fifth degree, with the answers in the opposite column.

SUBJECTS   ANSWERS

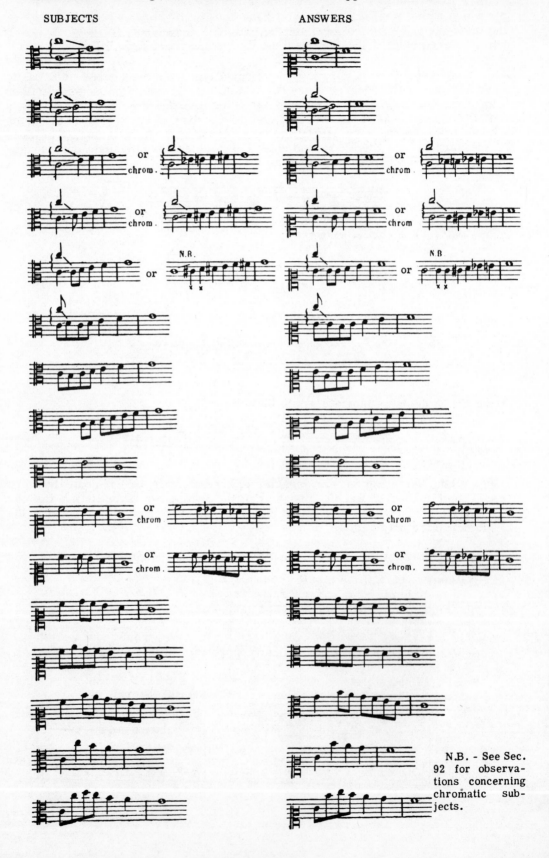

N.B. - See Sec. 92 for observations concerning chromatic subjects.

68. Every subject of this type can be represented by the following example which shows what the effect is at each diatonic or chromatic step of having the head of the subject begin on the tonic (or the mediant) and use various notes before going to the dominant (or to the seventh degree followed by the dominant):

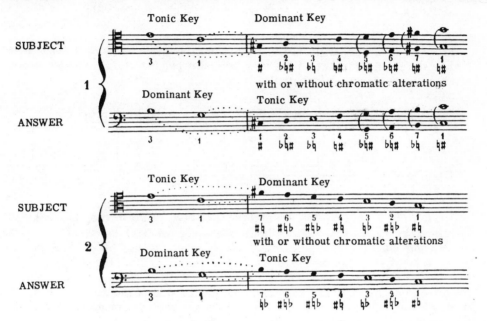

69. It has been stated above that when the subject goes to the dominant by way of the fourth degree of the main key, this fourth degree is treated harmonically (even though unaltered) as the leading tone of the dominant key. Actually, in such a case, the fourth degree is considered as the subtonic of the natural scale of the dominant[1] and is treated as if it were the leading tone. Note that in this scale the seventh degree is a natural tone.

Fourth Degree of the Main Key Considered as the Seventh Degree of the Dominant Key.

In any case, grant that the dominant of the main key, under these conditions, ceases to be a dominant and becomes the tonic of the dominant key. On this basis, it is impossible to consider the fourth degree as the root of the subdominant triad or the third of the supertonic triad of the main key, since neither of these chords can bring about a modulation to the dominant key and thus be part of the perfect cadence in that key.

70. Furthermore, in this way, the harmonies in this part of the answer are the same as those in the corresponding part of the subject. This comes about by applying the principle stated above: that every note which belongs to the dominant key in the subject should be answered by the corresponding degree of the main key.

What applies to the melody of the subject applies even more strongly to the harmonization of this melody.

---

1. The natural scale of the dominant is the scale which comes from the overtones of a vibrating string.

71. Consequently, the subject of a fugue cannot be analyzed from the point of view of tonality and harmony as if it were just any melodic phrase. In the head of a subject the role of the tonic of the dominant key attributed to the fifth degree also affects the degrees which immediately precede the fifth degree whenever these degrees are other than the first or third. The correctness of the answer depends on the rigor of this analysis.

72. For example, if the following subject is analyzed from a tonal point of view by considering it as just any melodic phrase, its first and second bars may be analyzed harmonically in E-flat.

But looking at it from the special point of view of the fugue, the dominant (B-flat) of the main key (second beat of the second bar) on which the first melodic movement (or head of the subject) ends, should be considered as the first degree of the dominant key. The result is that the subject modulates to the dominant, and thus cadences in this key. This cadence can be brought about only by an appropriate harmonization of the notes G and C in the third and fourth beats of the bar. This necessarily leads to its harmonization in the following manner with chords of the key of B-flat.

In the answer this harmonization will give the same chord progression in the key of E-flat, and the answer will be tonal.

In the third beat of the first bar of the subject, one could have equally well considered the G as the third of the subdominant chord of B-flat instead of the fifth of the supertonic chord of the same key. The corresponding harmony of the answer would have given the C of the third bar the role of third of the subdominant of E-flat. The cadence could have been brought about just as well whether the subdominant or the supertonic preceded the dominant. In each case the cadence ends with the tonic.

73. It goes without saying that, for purely musical reasons, one could use a real answer. "The heart has reasons which reason does not know." However, in the case at hand, the aforementioned harmonies in (b) and (c) are alone compatible with a true answer. Those in example (a) cannot be used here since they are entirely in the key of E-flat, and the subject modulates to the dominant. Note, however, that this way of looking at the subject harmonically is purely theoretical, having as its object only the tonal relationship between the subject and answer. The subject, considered alone, can be harmonized very differently.

74. When the dominant has been used as the first note of the subject (or after the tonic or mediant, followed or not by other degrees) the subject should return to the main key.

Return to the Main Key

Each note which follows the dominant, under these conditions, should be considered as belonging to the main key of the subject unless it is affected by an alteration characteristic of the dominant key or unless such alteration is implied in the harmony.

This is the same as saying that a subject can modulate to the dominant by the special rule for the fugue only once; and that, if it modulates there again, it can do so only by means of an alteration characteristic of the dominant key.

Examples:

Real Answer to a Tonal Subject

75. Besides chromatic subjects, there are a very limited number of cases involving subjects which go to the dominant using various steps of the scale, where one is justified in using a real answer. If the resulting tonal answer is unmusical, or if the melody of the subject becomes too much distorted, a real answer is called for.

Example:

For such a subject, it is obvious for the two reasons outlined above that the real answer, though contrary to the rule, is preferable.

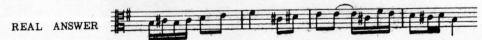

These cases, however, are rare. They are apt to occur when the first part of the subject is in the form of a sequence. Such cases are easily discerned.

76. For a subject such as the following the real answer is likewise preferable to the tonal answer because the latter distorts the melody of the subject too much.

It can be seen that, in the case of a tonal answer, the unaltered fourth degree of the main key must be considered as the subtonic of the natural scale of the dominant and must be represented in the answer by the leading tone of the main key. This changes the melodic character of the subject so much that it is better to use the real answer. Moreover, this is the best thing to do whenever a subject ends on the dominant preceded by the unaltered fourth degree of the main key.

77. A subject modulates to the dominant key whenever one of its notes is affected by an alteration characteristic of this key (Sec. 33) or whenever this alteration is implied in the harmony.

Modulation to the Dominant by Characteristic Alteration. Tonal Answer

In this case (Sections 28, 29):

Each fragment of the subject belonging to the main key is answered, step by step, alteration by alteration, in the dominant key, and vice versa:

Each fragment of the subject belonging to the dominant key is answered step by step, alteration by alteration, in the main key.

Example:

This subject is in F major: it ends on the dominant, and in addition it has the alteration characteristic of the dominant key in the next to last note. The natural before the B-flat, which is the fourth degree of the key of F, makes it the seventh degree of the key of C, the dominant of F.

The answer will therefore have the seventh degree followed by the first degree of the key of F and end in this way:

78. With this subject, however, it is obvious that modulation to the key of the dominant has taken place before the note characteristic of this key has been heard.

It is not always easy to determine the exact instant that modulation to the dominant takes place. In many cases one can find two or even several tonal interpretations of the subject all of which are more or less defensible. It is certain, nevertheless, that among the possible solutions of a given case, there is one to be preferred to the others.

Subjects Analyzed

79. We shall try to demonstrate the above by means of a tonal analysis of the preceding subject and of several similar ones.

Example:

SUBJECT

For the sake of discussion we shall assume that this subject can be divided into two distinct motives:

First Motive

Second Motive

The first motive begins on the tonic and does not go to the dominant, therefore we should consider it as belonging to the category of a real fugue, and should treat it in the answer as if the subject were composed solely of this motive.

By calculating the steps of this motive in relation to the first degree of F, we shall obtain the following answer:

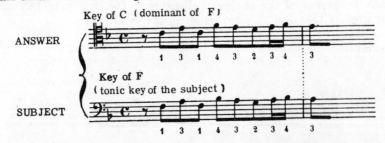

ANSWER

Key of C (dominant of F)

1   3   1   4   3   2   3   4   :   3

Key of F
(tonic key of the subject)

SUBJECT

1   3   1   4   3   2   3   4   3

80. The roots of the harmonies of the second motive are the following:

(appog)

(1)

Roots of the Harmonies

----

1. Either one of these notes is acceptable as the root.

It is obvious that the G, the root of the harmony of the second note of this motive, must have a major chord in the key of C. The implication, then, is that modulation to the dominant must begin on the first note of the second motive.

Since this motive is entirely in the dominant key of the subject, the answer will have the corresponding degrees of the tonic key of the subject.

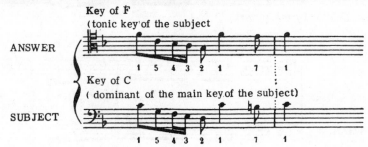

The combination of the two motives of the subject will have as its answer:

81. The following solutions have been offered on an examination. They are obviously false. To be convinced of it, all one has to do is compare them to the subject in terms of the harmonies that they imply in the subject. One can see the impossibility of justifying these harmonies tonally.

In this answer one is obliged to assume that the fragment of the subject indicated by the signs (+) is in the key of F since it has been answered by the corresponding degrees of the key of C. It is then impossible to understand why the seventh degree of this key of C is flatted, an alteration characteristic of the key of F. This alteration could be justified only if the subject had this form:

which is impossible musically.

82. In the same way the two following answers may be analyzed. You will see that from a harmonic and tonal point of view they cannot be justified.

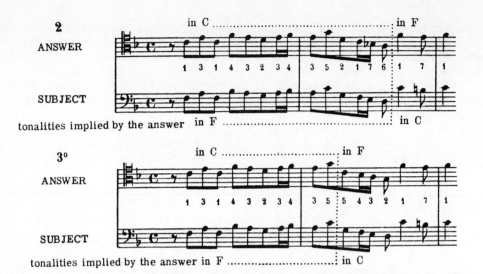

83. The following subject

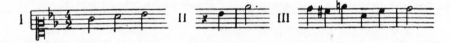

is in G minor. It begins on the first degree and modulates to the dominant key because it ends on the fifth degree and is preceded by a note with the alteration characteristic of the dominant key.

It can be divided into three melodic motives:

The first and second motives are obviously in the key of G minor.
Actually:
The first motive (head of the subject) goes from the tonic to the mediant and passes through the second degree. According to the rule, these notes should be assigned to the key of G minor (main key of the subject).

The second motive can have only the following harmony:

The answer to the first two motives together, therefore, will be:

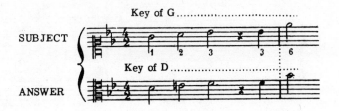

84. The only thing left to discuss is the tonal role to be attributed to the initial D in the third motive

since, obviously, the last five notes of the subject are in the key of D minor, the dominant of the subject. Actually the C-sharp (fourth degree of G) and the E (sixth degree of G) have the alterations characteristic of the key of D; the subject ends on the dominant and there is an obvious modulation to the key of D minor.

The first note of the third motive can be considered only as the root, third, or fifth of the chord:

1. It is certainly not the root of a D minor chord since the preceding E is the third of the subdominant chord of G and these two chords cannot be juxtaposed;

Neither is it the root of the major triad on the fifth degree of the key of G minor since the tonality of D minor cannot be established by a chord of D major;

2. For the same reasons it is not the third of the B-flat major triad on the sixth degree of the key of D minor.

3. One is therefore obliged to consider this note D as the fifth of the chord of G minor which becomes, because of the C-sharp immediately after it, the subdominant of D minor. Consequently the D must be considered as the first degree of the key of D minor. The third motive of the subject therefore has as the roots of its harmonies:

Roots of the
Harmonies

and as an answer:

which gives the following answer for the whole subject:

Dominant or Seventh Degree Ending the Subject. Tonal Answer

85. A subject modulates to the dominant key when it ends:
a) on the dominant[1] (Sec. 37).

In this case:

The dominant is considered as the first degree of the dominant key and the answer ends on the first degree of the main key.

b) on the seventh degree (unaltered in the minor mode) of the main key (Sec. 38).

In this case:

This seventh degree (unaltered in the minor mode) is considered as the third degree of the dominant key and the answer ends on the third degree of the main key.

Examples:

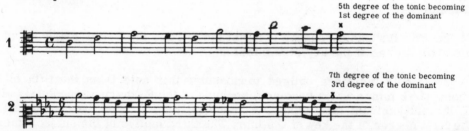

86. To find the answer for these subjects, there are good grounds for applying to them the same procedures of analysis as to the subjects treated in the preceding section.

First:

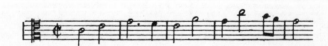

This subject can be divided into three motives:

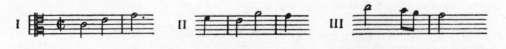

1. Even when the dominant is preceded by the unaltered fourth degree of the main key, which then becomes the subtonic of the dominant key, and which is answered by the leading tone of the main key (Section 76).

The first motive, according to the rule, calls for the following answer:

The subject, having modulated to the dominant, should, to be tonal, revert to the main key. Now, in the second motive, there is no alteration characteristic of the dominant key, nor is such alteration implied in the harmony. This motive, therefore, belongs in its entirety to the main tonality of the subject and gives the following answer:

In the third motive, the final note should be considered as the first degree of the dominant key. This implies that the modulation takes place on the first note of the motive, the C, which will then have to be considered as the fourth degree of the key of G. The answer is as follows:

and for the whole subject:

87. Second: analyzing this subject in the same manner:

one finds that the last motive belongs in its entirety to the key of E-flat, the dominant of the main key.

In reality the last note, G, should, according to the rule, be considered as the third degree of the dominant key, E-flat; as a result, the B-flat and A-flat which precede it imply in their harmony a D, an alteration characteristic of the key of E-flat.

Therefore the answer will be:

The answers for the following subjects will be found in the same way:

88. The reciprocal imitation of tonic key by dominant key makes the answer (whose tonic is the dominant of the subject) seem to modulate to the key of its own subdominant whenever it imitates a fragment of the subject modulating to the dominant.

Mutation

From each of the preceding examples it can be seen that the answer undergoes a change in relation to the subject whenever it modulates to the dominant or returns to the main key.

This modification is called m u t a t i o n.

Mutation is brought about by the removal or addition of the interval of a second between two notes in the answer, one considered as belonging to the key of the first degree, the other to the fifth degree of the subject.

89. In certain cases mutation in the answer brings about an imitation of the subject by oblique motion. In no case, however, can imitation of the subject by inversion be permitted.

90. To lay down a hard and fast rule: mutation produces, in the answer, the removal of the interval of a second (major or minor depending on the mode)

1. When the subject, at its beginning, goes from the tonic to the dominant (or to one of the degrees of the dominant key) by ascending motion;

Example:

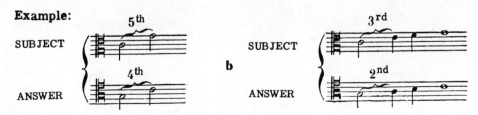

2. When the subject, at its beginning, goes from the dominant to the ton-ic (or to one of the degrees of the main key) by descending motion;

Example:

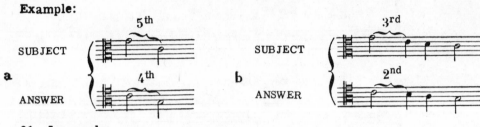

91. Inversely:

Mutation produces, in the answer, the addition of the interval of a second (major or minor depending on the mode):

1. When the subject, at its beginning, goes from the tonic to the domi-nant (or to one of the degrees of the dominant key) by descending motion;

Example:

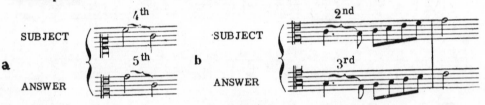

3. When the subject, at its beginning, goes from the dominant to the tonic (or to one of the degrees of the main key) by ascending motion.

Example:

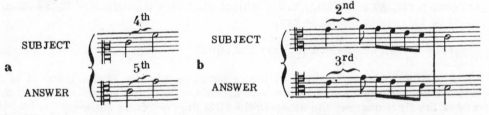

The same thing occurs in the same way whenever the subject modulates from the main key to the dominant key and vice versa.

Observations concerning Chromatic Subjects.

92. Imitation of the subject by inversion would occur with a chromatic subject going at its beginning from the dominant to the tonic by descending motion.

It would occur in the answer to the chromatic alteration of the fourth degree of the main key when it immediately follows the fifth degree of the main key, taken as the first degree of the dominant key.

It may also occur with a chromatic subject going at its beginning from the tonic to the dominant by ascending motion:

In this case it comes about with the answer to the chromatic alteration of the fourth degree of the dominant key when it immediately follows the first degree of the main key, and when the subject uses all the degrees conjunctly from the first to the fifth.

93. To understand properly the mechanism of the answer of a subject belonging to one of the two preceding types, each one of them must be considered with the chromatics omitted:

Example:

Here is the answer (Sec. 43) for the subject thus reduced to its diatonic framework:

Now, in the subject, one can interpolate a chromatic step between the first and second note, but it is not possible in the answer where the second note is a repetition of the first. In the answer, one is therefore obliged to repeat this same note until one reaches the unaltered fourth degree of the dominant key,

Example:

and one is obliged to answer a raised degree by an unaltered degree, so that the imitation will be by oblique motion.

94. Doing the same thing for a subject going directly to the dominant by ascending chromatic motion brings about the same result for the answer.

Example:

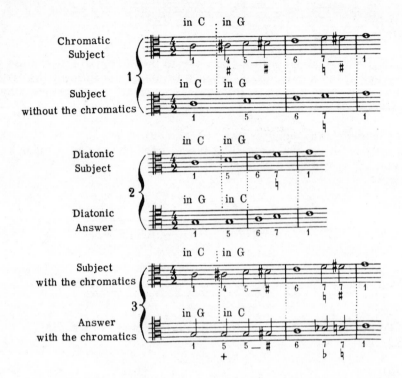

Here one can see that, in the answer, the fifth degree of the main key (first degree of the dominant key) must be repeated because a chromatic half-step cannot be interpolated between two notes of the same pitch.

On the other hand, this distortion no longer occurs in the answer when the subject takes a form like the following, for the imitation of the stepwise portion of the subject is now direct. The answers to subjects of this type must be as follows, in accordance with the general rule:

Example:

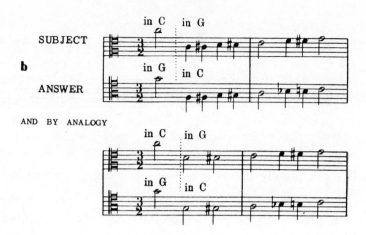

Note, however, the observation made below (Sec. 97) with regard to the real answer in similar cases.

95. The rule is the same when the subject, having modulated to the dominant key returns to the tonic or the mediant by chromatic motion:

Example:

or if, having proceeded from the dominant to the tonic, it returns to the dominant by chromatic motion to revert chromatically to the tonic or mediant:

Example:

96. It is a completely different matter when the chromatic motion of the subject:

a) stops or returns to the mediant or the tonic before reaching the dominant,

b) uses any other degree immediately after the tonic except the raised first degree of the main key or the lowered second degree of the main key.

In these cases the answer follows the rules given above (Sec. 16).

Example:

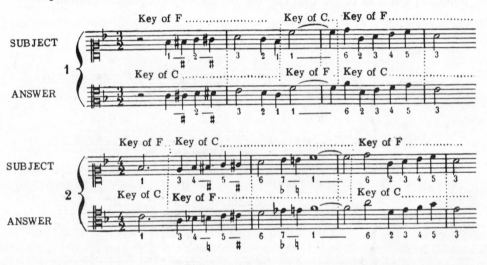

97. In any case, when a subject goes directly and chromatically from the dominant to the tonic by descending motion or from the tonic to the dominant by ascending motion, a real answer is preferable if the tonal answer distorts the subject too much.

Example:

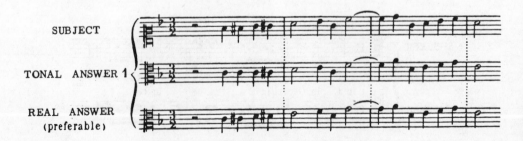

98. When the chromatic subject ascends from the dominant to the tonic or descends from the tonic to the dominant, its character is better preserved by a tonal answer than in the preceding cases. Nevertheless, it is still better to have a real answer.

99. From everything that has been said above we may draw the following theoretical conclusions:

1. A subject may begin only on the tonic, mediant, or dominant.

2. A subject must end on the tonic, mediant, dominant, or seventh degree (unaltered in the minor mode).

In free composition it sometimes happens that a fugue subject may begin on some other degree than the ones listed above. The composer of such a subject can interpret it as he wishes from the point of view of tonality and of the answer to be given to it.

Nevertheless, on the basis of the rules outlined above, a rational interpretation which will allow for a logical answer can be found for every subject of this type.

100. When a subject in the major mode begins on the seventh degree, this seventh degree will always be considered as the third degree of the dominant key.

Therefore, it will be answered by the third degree of the main key as if the subject began in the dominant key.

Observations Concerning some Exceptional Forms of Subjects.

Subject beginning on the Seventh degree. (Major Mode)

Example:

An answer which uses the seventh degree of the dominant key is illogical both from a harmonic and tonal point of view. The seventh degree of the main key must be the third of the dominant chord and can be answered only by the third of the tonic chord; since the fifth degree of the main key, at the beginning of a subject, is always considered as the first degree of the dominant key.

This subject should therefore be treated as if it began on the dominant since the roots of the harmonies are the same in both cases:

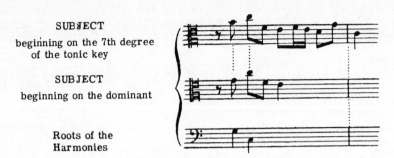

SUBJECT

beginning on the 7th degree of the tonic key

SUBJECT

beginning on the dominant

Roots of the Harmonies

Subject beginning on the Seventh Degree (Minor Mode)

101. When a subject in the minor mode begins on the raised seventh degree, this seventh degree will always be considered as the leading tone of the main key. It will, therefore, be answered by the leading tone of the dominant key.

Example:

SUBJECT

Key of C♯ min ....

ANSWER

Key of G♯ min ....

This raised seventh degree cannot be considered as the third of the triad on the fifth degree of C-sharp minor, because that triad is minor.

In the minor mode it is absolutely impossible to begin a subject on the unaltered seventh degree of the main key.

Subject beginning on the Raised Fourth Degree

102. If a subject begins on the raised fourth degree of the main key, this degree will always be considered as the leading tone of the dominant key.

It will be answered by the seventh degree (raised in the minor mode) of the main key.

Example:

SUBJECT

Key of C .... Key of F ....

ANSWER

Key of F .... Key of C ....

103. If a subject begins on the second, the unaltered fourth, or the sixth degrees of the main key, it will be considered as beginning in the tonic key. One will treat the first note as being in this key and refer to the rules listed above (Sections 35 ff.) for the rest of the answer.

Example:

It is almost impossible to begin a subject on the fourth or sixth degrees of a key without evoking a feeling of the tonality for which these notes would be the first degree. One must avoid subjects that begin in this way. Composing one's own subjects will make one realize quite easily how uncertain the tonality and mode of a subject are when it begins on any other degree than the tonic, mediant, or dominant.

104. To sum up:

I

The subject of a fugue does not modulate when it begins and ends on the tonic or the mediant and does not go to the fifth degree, or uses the fifth degree only secondarily as a passing tone or an auxiliary tone, or in a sequence.

II

A subject modulates to the dominant key when it begins on the tonic or the mediant and goes to the fifth degree either directly or with various steps of the tonic key or the dominant key in between.

III

The subject of a fugue modulates to the dominant key when it begins on the dominant or ends on the dominant or the seventh degree (unaltered in the minor mode).

In this case, the dominant of the subject becomes the tonic of the dominant key, and the seventh degree of the subject (unaltered in the minor mode) is considered as the third degree of the dominant key.

IV

When the subject begins on the tonic or mediant and goes to the dominant (or to the seventh degree immediately followed by the dominant) with various other degrees in between, all these degrees are considered as being in the main key of the subject if the note immediately preceding the dominant is the mediant or the tonic.

V

The subject modulates to the dominant key whenever it uses an alteration characteristic of this key, or whenever such alteration is implied in the harmony.

VI

Once the dominant is used as tonic of the key of the fifth degree (either as the first note of the subject or in the head of the subject after the tonic or mediant of the main key), all notes which follow must be considered as being in the main key. That is, the subject can modulate thereafter to the dominant key only if an alteration characteristic of this key appears before one of the notes or is implied in the harmony.

VII

Each step which is in the main key in the subject must be answered (with the alterations which affect it) by the corresponding step of the dominant key (imitation limited to the fifth above or the fourth below).

And vice versa:

Each step which is in the dominant key in the subject must be answered (with the alterations which affect it) by the corresponding step of the main key (imitation limited to the fourth above or the fifth below).

CHAPTER IV

The Countersubject

105. **C o u n t e r s u b j e c t** is the name given to that part of the fugue, written in counterpoint invertible at the octave or the fifteenth, which is introduced shortly after the subject and accompanies it thereafter at each one of its entries.

Definition

106. The characteristics of a good countersubject are the following:

1. The modulations of the countersubject should correspond to those of the subject, but there should be no resemblance between the two either in melody or in rhythm. Despite the differences, however, the countersubject should be in the same style as the subject.

Characteristics of the Countersubject.

A countersubject should not be, in character or mood, dissimilar to the subject it accompanies. No more than, in any composition, would one give a light, merry accompaniment to a serious melody.

2. Both subject and countersubject should be able to serve as a good harmonic bass for each other.

The above point is essential. It must never be forgotten that, in the course of a fugue, subject and countersubject appear alternately in all parts. It is therefore necessary that each of them should be able to serve as a good harmonic bass.

3. The countersubject should always enter after the subject, and insofar as possible, it should begin immediately after the head of the subject.

The purpose of this rule is to enable the subject to maintain its dominance and to avoid any confusion such as would result from simultaneous entries.

The subject of a fugue may have as many countersubjects as there are vocal or instrumental parts in addition to the one which has the subject. Thus one must take care that the countersubjects, in a fugue with more than one countersubject, should enter in succession and not simultaneously.

When there is more than one countersubject, each one should have its own distinct melody, different from the melodies of the other countersubjects and from the melody of the subject itself. The countersubjects should not imitate each other any more than they would the subject.

Example:

4. Every strong beat of the bar should have a note belonging either to the subject or the countersubject.

The countersubject should not have the same note values in the same places as the subject. Similarly, if the subject has rests, the countersubject should fill them; and likewise, the countersubject should have rests only when the subject has a melodic movement.

Example:

5. The harmonies implied by the countersubject should be as rich and varied as possible.

For this reason it is necessary to use suspensions as often as possible. On the other hand, changing the harmonies too many times in a bar should be avoided. Finally, one should treat as nonharmonic tones all those notes whose harmonization is not absolutely necessary.

Example:

N.B. Whenever a note at the end of a bar is repeated at the beginning of the following bar immediately after a rest and descends one step, it should be considered as a suspension and should be treated harmonically as if the syncopated note had been sustained. One should treat the fourth and fifth bars of the example above as if the melody were as follows:

107. When the countersubject accompanies the answer of a subject which does not modulate (real fugue), it does not undergo any change. It is simply transposed to the key of the answer.

If the subject does modulate (tonal fugue), the countersubject accompanying the answer has modifications corresponding to the changes which the answer has undergone.

Therefore, there is mutation in the countersubject that corresponds to the mutation of the answer.

108. When a subject calls for a mutation at its very beginning, the countersubject is not begun until immediately after the mutation.

Mutation in the Counter-subject.

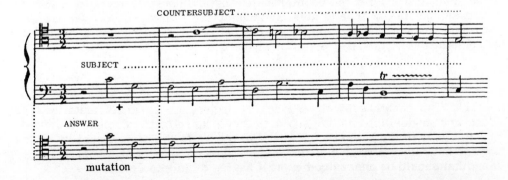

109. If, for some reason or other, the countersubject is begun before the first mutation of the subject, the same rules of mutation are applied to it as to the subject when this countersubject accompanies the answer. Thus, the mutations are the same for both.

Example:

The numbers over the notes indicate the degrees of the scale.

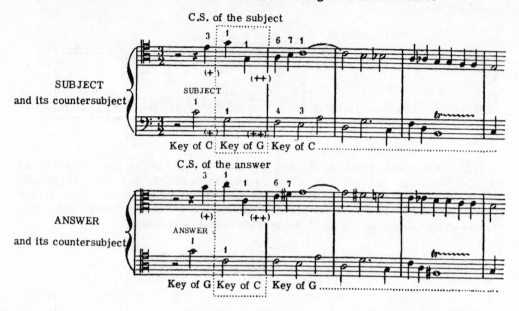

In the head of the countersubject here there are two mutations corresponding to changes of intervals (+) of the answer in relation to the subject. The countersubject of the answer has an interval of a second to answer an interval of a third (+) at the beginning of the countersubject of the subject; the opposite occurs at the sign (++) where an interval of a third answers an interval of a second in the countersubject of the subject. In this case, the subject and answer have mutations inverse to those of the countersubject in the sense that where a step is added between two notes of the answer, a step is removed from the countersubject, and vice versa.

110. However, in many, many cases, almost insurmountable difficulties arise from introducing the countersubject before the first mutation, and, in any case, one is not free to give the head of the countersubject the melodic form that one would like. Therefore, it is better not to introduce the countersubject until after the first mutation of the answer.

111. The countersubject, moreover, undergoes as many mutations as there are modulations in the subject. Since the effects of these mutations are felt only in the answers, one must never write the countersubject on the answer but rather always use the subject when composing it. This is something that should be understood without having to go into detail.

Use of Suspensions 112. The removal or addition of a step which mutation produces in the answer often makes it difficult to use suspensions in the countersubject. Suspensions which work in the countersubject of the subject may not have any resolution in the countersubject of the answer.

One may sometimes circumvent this problem by repeating a note in the countersubject if mutation involves the contraction of an interval by one step.

Example:

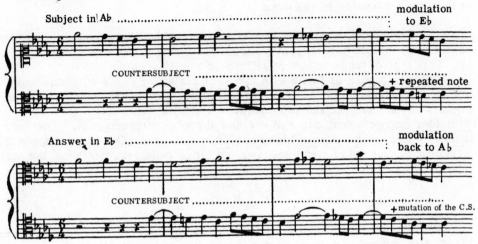

From this example it can be seen that a mutation which contracts an interval by one step in the answer, adds one step in the same place in the countersubject.

If the countersubject had had the suspension without the repeated note

one would have had for the countersubject of the answer:

which would have produced the dissonance of a second without resolution.

It is true that this passage could have been written in this way:

However, aside from the fact that this form would have produced a very awkward harmonic progression, it would have spoiled the melodic line of the countersubject too much. Rather than have a consonance with an insipid, ineffectual harmony, it is better to make use of the device pointed out above of repeating a note in the countersubject of the subject. One will note that in this case, as in all analogous cases, the resolution of the dissonance does not come on the same beat of the measure in the countersubject of the answer as in the countersubject of the subject; but that is not important. The main point is that the suspension is resolved.

Nomenclature of Fugues

113. Formerly, a simple fugue was one in which the countersubject was replaced by simple counterpoints varied according to the will of the composer. This type of fugue is now practiced only in free composition.

A double fugue, or fugue with two subjects was a fugue with one subject and one countersubject. A triple fugue, or fugue with three subjects was a fugue with one subject and two countersubjects; a quadruple fugue, or fugue with four subjects had one subject and three countersubjects. The terms double, triple, or quadruple fugue are no longer used. One says simply that a fugue has one subject and one, two, or three countersubjects as the case may be.

114. When a fugue has two or three countersubjects, they should be combined with the subject in accordance with the rules of triple or quadruple counterpoint, respectively.

115. Although it is possible to compose a good fugue without a countersubject, it is impossible to compose a good one with a poor countersubject.

The composition of the countersubject is therefore of the greatest importance. We shall outline below, a practical way of composing a good countersubject.

Construction of the Countersubject.

116. Once the subject has been selected, it must be analyzed harmonically before anything else can be done. Then the framework of the countersubject is built by selecting the best of the chord tones which can be inverted with the subject, that is, those chord tones which provide the best bass for the subject and for which the subject can serve as a good bass.

Now that one has a preliminary outline of the countersubject, it remains only to give it the form and character that is best in keeping with the melody of the subject.

Example:

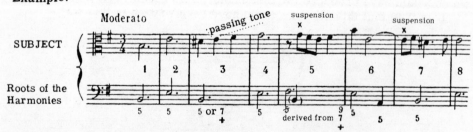

117. The subject above is composed of eight bars.

In a preceding section we have seen that the countersubject should begin immediately after the head of the subject. Therefore we shall set aside the first bar and begin it with the second.

1. **Second Bar.**
Of the three notes contained in the harmony of this bar,

two, E and G, can be inverted with the note E of the subject. Both of them are equally good as basses, and, inversely, the subject can serve both of them as a good bass. Therefore, either one is equally suitable and can be used.

2. **Third Bar.**

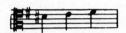

To avoid too many changes of harmony, we shall consider the E of the second beat as a passing tone. At the same time we shall eliminate as a chord member the seventh of the dominant, which, necessitating a preparation, would require the harmonization of the E of the second beat. This seventh, moreover, because it is not prepared in the preceding bar, cannot be used as a chord member with the first note (D-sharp) of the bar. Therefore, as notes that can be inverted with the D-sharp and F-sharp of the bar, we have only the third (D-sharp) of the chord or the fifth (F-sharp). The D-sharp of the first beat, however, cannot be doubled harmonically as it is the leading tone. In the countersubject, therefore, we are limited to the F-sharp for the first beat; and, for the third beat, we have a choice between the D-sharp and the F-sharp. At first glance, we shall pick the D-sharp which will give us an exchange of notes with the subject.

3. **Fourth Bar.**

Harmony

The three notes of the chord can be inverted with the note G of the subject. They are equally good as bass notes, although the root or the third are preferable.

118. Taking an overall picture of the four bars, we have the following outline for our countersubject:

Continuing in the same manner for the other four bars, we will get the following outline for the countersubject:

5

Taking bars three and four together, however, we can see that if we sustain the F-sharp in the third bar for the three beats, we will be able to suspend it on the first beat of the fourth bar. This suspension will give us a richer harmony:

The same thing can be done in the sixth bar, in which we can suspend the A of the preceding bar over to the first beat and resolve it to G;

so that, for the entire countersubject, we obtain the following:

119. In its above form, the countersubject can suffice harmonically. But from the point of view of contrapuntal elaboration, it would offer no resources. Only the sixth bar has an expressive melodic movement in keeping with the character of the subject.

It is therefore necessary to rework this sketch; in short, to make of it a musical phrase which, like a different melody in the same style, can accompany the melody of the subject without resembling it rhythmically or melodically.

120. First of all, in the second bar we shall avoid beginning the countersubject on the first beat, so that its entry may be more marked. And since we have a choice between the two notes E and G, we shall be able to use them in succession so that all beats of the bar are articulated. It is, in fact, necessary for the countersubject to strike the beats which the subject does not strike and vice versa; it is useless for the countersubject always to have melodic movement at the same time as the subject.

In other words, subject and countersubject must avoid a succession of notes of the same value sounded simultaneously.

For the same reason, we shall strike the third beat of the fourth bar with either G or B, and, in the next to the last bar, we shall use on the third beat the seventh (A) which will connect the B of the first beat with the G of the first beat of the eighth bar.

We shall therefore have a choice between the two forms below for the countersubject, with very little difference between them. Both are equally good harmonically, although the first is preferable melodically:

121. Certain subjects can be harmonized only chromatically. By treating them otherwise one runs the risk of committing the very grave mistake—unpardonable to a musician-of treating a subject belonging to the major mode as if it were in the minor mode and vice versa.

Chromatic Countersubjects.

122. In the subject:

it is obvious that the second bar cannot have F as the root of its harmony since the A-flat, an altered note, would make that harmony belong to the minor mode. It is therefore necessary to give this subject a harmony such as the following which alone will make possible a good countersubject.

123. It is the same for the subject below, which at one point (third bar) modulates from the main key to the subdominant key (minor mode). It would be inexcusable to suppose that this subject, which is in the minor mode, could end up in the major mode.

124. Therefore, it is useful in the harmonic analysis of a subject always to be concerned with the possibility of a chromatic progression. When such a possibility exists, it unquestionably provides the countersubject with the greatest harmonic richness. For that very reason alone, it should be preferred to any other.

125. Here are a few other examples, in tabular form, of the various steps in writing a countersubject:

The same countersubject (inverted at the fifteenth) accompanying the answer:

The same countersubject accompanying the answer:

The same countersubject accompanying the answer

Above, in an analytical form, are the successive operations in the construction of a countersubject. With experience and practice, one can acquire an intuitive overall conception of the process. Then the notes of the countersubject will come to mind immediately, without there being any need, except in certain especially subtle cases, of going through this procedure of formal analysis, a process which now takes place instinctively.

To sum up: It can be seen that, for any given subject, all the good countersubjects have as their bases the same harmonic elements. They differ from each other only in the rhythm or melody attributed to these elements by the imagination of the individual.

CHAPTER V

The Exposition of the Fugue

Definitions

126. At the beginning of a fugue, the subject is presented in one of the parts, then the answer in another part. A third voice has the subject again, to be followed by the answer as the fourth entry.

The ensemble of these four successive entries together constitutes the exposition.

127. No matter how many vocal or instrumental parts a fugue may have, the exposition never has less than four entries.

Entry of the Countersubject.

128. The subject must always alternate with the answer.

One or more countersubjects may be introduced as early as the first entry of the subject, but to insure good comprehension of the themes on which the fugue is based, it is better to introduce them in succession and to present the subject by itself. The countersubject is then introduced with the entry of the answer. This arrangement has the advantage of giving more prominence to both subject and countersubject.

129. If there are several countersubjects, the first can be introduced with the second entry and the others, successively, with the third and fourth entries. This order of presentation will make it easier to follow the developments of the main theme and accessory themes in the course of the fugue.

130. If, however, the subject has long note-values, or if it does not have a very pronounced melodic character, one may use one or more countersubjects as early as the first entry in order to heighten interest at the beginning of the fugue and avoid an otherwise cold and uninspired effect.

Subject assigned to a Corresponding Voice.

131. A subject which is designated for one voice may be transferred to the voice of corresponding tessitura. That is to say, a subject written for bass may also be presented in the alto, and vice versa. Similarly, a subject written for tenor may also be presented by the soprano, and vice versa. But in the exposition, a subject designated for tenor or soprano should never enter in the bass or alto, or vice versa.

132. If the countersubject is used with the first entry of the subject, it should be presented preferably in the voice of corresponding tessitura.

If the countersubject is to be introduced first as accompaniment to the answer, it is well to have it in the part which has just presented the subject.

(This observation applies only to the case of a fugue with only one countersubject.)

133. The answer should be introduced as soon as the subject has been completely presented.

Rather frequently, however, this rule cannot be observed either because of the rhythm of the subject or because of the modulation of the answer, which prevents the two tonalities from being linked correctly.

Example:

It is obvious that, here, introducing the answer immediately after the last note of the subject would completely distort the rhythm, since the strong beats of the answer would not jibe with those of the subject. From a purely musical point of view, this rhythmic distortion cannot be permitted.

134. The rest of the bar is, in this case, filled in with a **codetta**.

Codetta of the Subject.

A codetta is a melodic passage written in single or double counterpoint which serves to introduce the entry of the answer and which is continued until the entry of the countersubject. A short rest, however, may precede the entry of the countersubject.

This codetta should be in the style of the subject and countersubject so that the latter is the natural consequence of the codetta, just as the codetta should follow the subject logically.

135. The codetta, actually, just like any other melodic or rhythmic figure in the exposition, becomes an integral part of the fugue and becomes a source of material for the subsequent development of the subject.

If the note which ends the subject and the one which begins the answer, even though consonant with each other, do not belong to the same tonality, and if the subject ends on the beat on which the answer should be introduced, then a codetta must be added. An example of such a case will be found in one of the expositions to be presented below (Sec. 156).

In certain cases a codetta is appended to the subject before the answer enters even though the latter could be introduced on the last note of the subject. There is an example in Sec. 172 (eighth bar) in which the codetta is added for the sake of musical feeling and in order to avoid a unison.

Purely musical considerations may also lead to the omission of a codetta which at first sight might seem necessary (see exposition in Sections 160-161). Under such circumstances one can be guided only by one's own feelings, for it is impossible to anticipate cases of this kind and to lay down fixed rules concerning them.

Second Codetta.

136. With an answer that enters on the last note of the subject, it often happens that the third entry cannot be made immediately after the second. A second codetta is then added between the second and third entries.

This codetta can be more extended and can consist of two or three bars in accordance with the tempo of the fugue. If one fears that the subject and its countersubject do not furnish enough material for subsequent development, one can take advantage of the codetta to introduce new melodic and rhythmic figures which may be used later. But one is absolutely obligated to use them later to fill in parts which make use of neither the subject nor the countersubject.

The above procedure is rather frequently used even if alternate entries of subject and answer can be made without interruption.

Unison to be Avoided.

137. One must avoid a unison between the last note of the subject and the first note of the answer.

In such a case the first entry of the subject is changed to the voice of corresponding tessitura (soprano to tenor, alto to bass).

Example: the subject appears in the alto

and produces a unison with the first note of the answer; this subject is transferred to the bass, the corresponding voice of the alto:

thus the first note of the answer is the octave above the last note of the subject instead of forming a unison with it.

Another way of avoiding a unison of this type is to add a codetta to the
subject (see example, Sec. 172).

138. When the part which first introduces the subject has finished it,   **Free Voices**
another part presents the answer. Meanwhile, the first part continues with
a simple counterpoint or free part which is interrupted by a short rest just
before the entry of the countersubject. The countersubject may, however,
follow this counterpoint without interruption.
    Once the answer is finished, a third part has the subject while the voice
which had presented the answer takes up the countersubject in its turn, just
as the first part had done. The latter continues to accompany this third entry with a free part in simple counterpoint.
    Then the fourth voice presents the answer accompanied by the counter-
subject in the voice which has just had the subject. The two other parts have
simple counterpoints in the same style as the subject and countersubject.

139. These counterpoints, or free parts, should be of positive melodic
interest and not be simple harmonic fill-ins.
    As much as possible, from the very beginning, these free parts should
be written in a style of free imitation.

140. If the fugue is in two parts, each voice will present both the subject   **Exposition in**
and answer. The voice which has the subject in the first entry will have the   **Two Voices**
answer at the fourth entry, and, as a result, the voice which had the answer
at the second entry will also have the third entry (the subject).

141. In an exposition in three parts, the voice which has the subject at   **Exposition**
the first entry will have the answer at the fourth entry. The two other voices **with More**
will have the second entry (answer) and the third entry (subject).   **Than Two**
    With more than three parts, each voice can be used only once, either for   **Voices**
subject or answer.
    The following illustrations give the various dispositions for the succes-
sive entries of subject and answer for expositions in two, three, or four parts:

142.

A

**Exposition
with One
Countersub-
ject.**

Models of expositions with one countersubject entering after the subject
(that is, not before the second entry)

1. In Two Parts

N⁰ 1.

a)

①			④
Subject	Countersubject	Countersubject	Answer
	②	③	
	Answer	Subject	Countersubject

N⁰ 2.

b)

	②	③	
	Answer	Subject	Countersubject
①			④
Subject	Countersubject	Countersubject	Answer

Note: in a two-part fugue the two dispositions above are the only ones possible; that is to say, the subject must appear once by itself, without being
accompanied by the countersubject.

143. ### 2. In Three Parts

N⁰ 1.

c)

①			④
Subject	Countersubject	Free Part	Answer
	②		
	Answer	Countersubject	Free Part
		③	
		Subject	Countersubject

N⁰ 2.

d)

		③	
		Subject	Countersubject
①			④
Subject	Countersubject	Free Part	Answer
	②		
	Answer	Countersubject	Free Part

N⁰ 3.

e)

		③	
		Subject	Countersubject
	②		
	Answer	Countersubject	Free Part
①			④
Subject	Countersubject	Free Part	Answer

N⁰ 4.

f)

	②		
	Answer	Countersubject	Free Part
①			④
Subject	Countersubject	Free Part	Answer
		③	
		Subject	Countersubject

3. In Four Parts

144.

Nº 1.

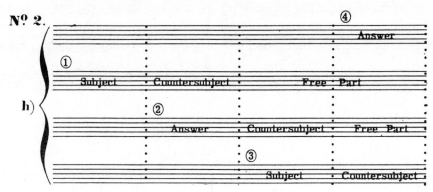

Nº 2.

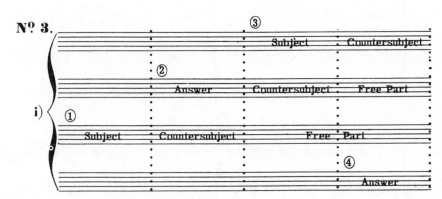

Nº 3.

Nº 4.

B.

145. Models of expositions with one countersubject entering simultaneously with the first entry of the subject.

1. In Three Parts

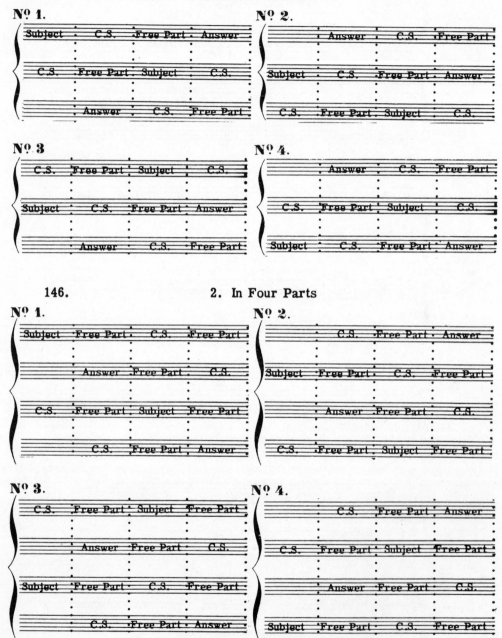

146.   2. In Four Parts

The free parts should be separated from the entries of the subject, the
answer, or the countersubject by a more or less prolonged rest. (Cf. Sections 172 ff.) In order not to complicate the following illustrations, the free
parts have not been indicated; but it is understood that they always continue
each entry of the subject, answer, or countersubject as shown in the illustration above.

Exposition with One Countersubject (cont.)

147. Dispositions to be avoided; the voices are not used in their normal order. These dispositions, however, may be used in certain cases when the tessitura of subject and answer lends itself thereto.

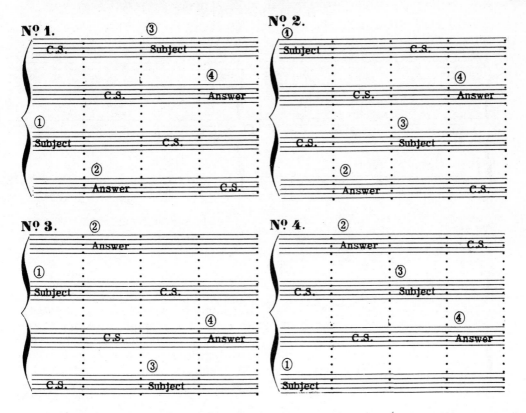

148. Dispositions other than those illustrated above are forbidden because they use subject and answer in voices of similar tessitura.

Example:

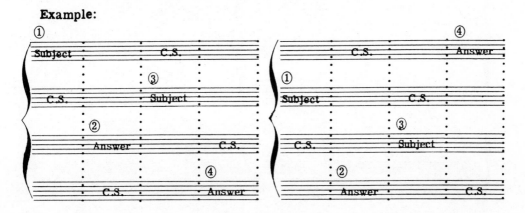

149. Also to be avoided are those dispositions in which one would use the subject and its countersubject simultaneously in two voices of dissimilar tessitura, as, for example, the subject in the tenor and its countersubject in the bass, the answer in the alto and its countersubject in the soprano, etc. That is, in every case one should assign the countersubject to the voice of tessitura corresponding to the one which presents the subject at the same time.

Exposition with Two Countersubjects.

150.

C.

Models of Expositions with Two Countersubjects

1. In Three Parts

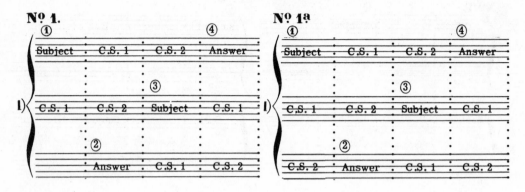

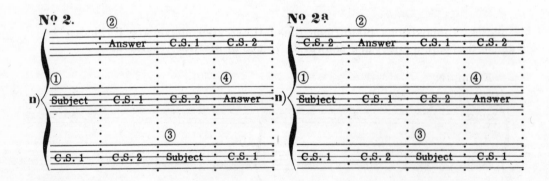

Note; this last disposition should be used only in exceptional circumstances, in cases for example, in which the second part would not be apt to use the countersubject of the subject because its tessitura is either too high or too low.

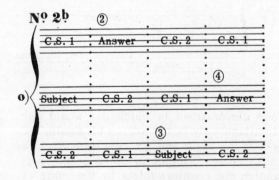

Same observation as for no. 1b.

Exposition with Two Countersubjects (cont.)

No. 3.

p)
③
C.S. 1 C.S. 2 Subject C.S. 1
① ④
Subject C.S. 1 C.S. 2 Answer
②
Answer C.S. 1 C.S. 2

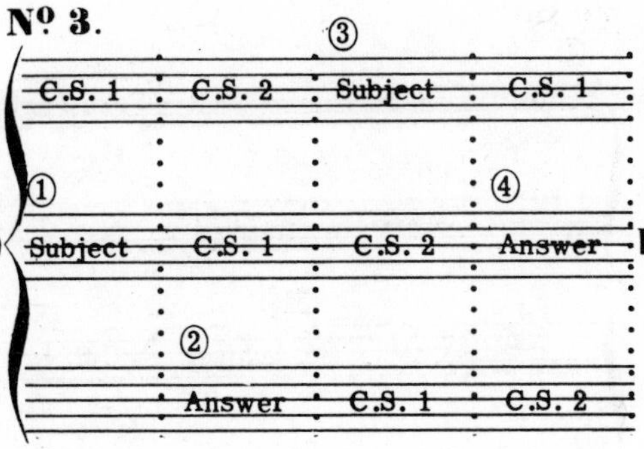

No. 3a

p)
③
C.S. 1 C.S. 2 Subject C.S. 1
① ④
Subject C.S. 1 C.S. 2 Answer
②
C.S. 2 Answer C.S. 1 C.S. 2

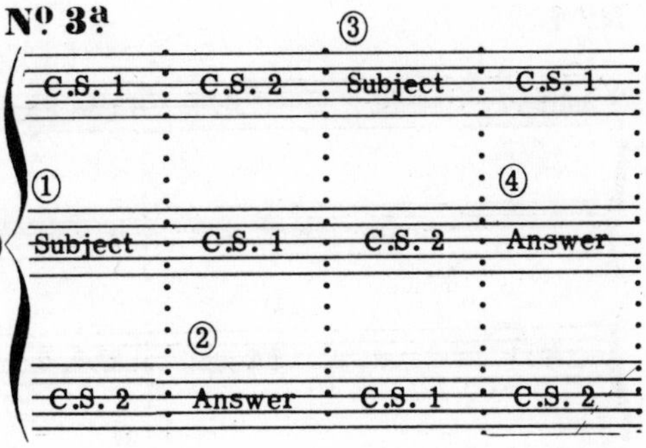

No. 3b

q)
③
C.S. 2 C.S. 1 Subject C.S. 2
① ④
Subject C.S. 2 C.S. 1 Answer
②
C.S. 1 Answer C.S. 2 C.S. 1

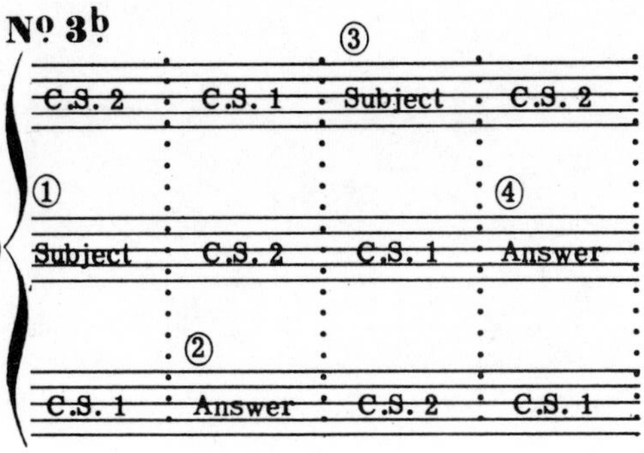

Same observation as for no. 1b.

No. 4.

r)
②
Answer C.S. 1 C.S. 2
③
C.S. 1 C.S. 2 Subject C.S. 1
① ④
Subject C.S. 1 C.S. 2 Answer

No. 4a

r)
②
C.S. 2 Answer C.S. 1 C.S. 2
③
C.S. 1 C.S. 2 Subject C.S. 1
① ④
Subject C.S. 1 C.S. 2 Answer

No. 4b

s)
②
C.S. 1 Answer C.S. 2 C.S. 1
③
C.S. 2 C.S. 1 Subject C.S. 2
① ④
Subject C.S. 2 C.S. 1 Answer

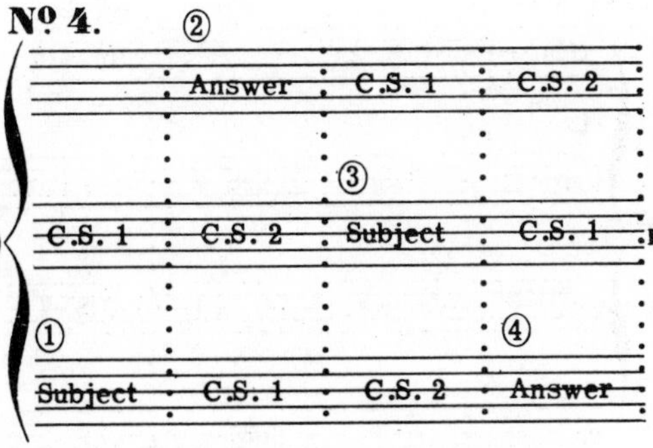

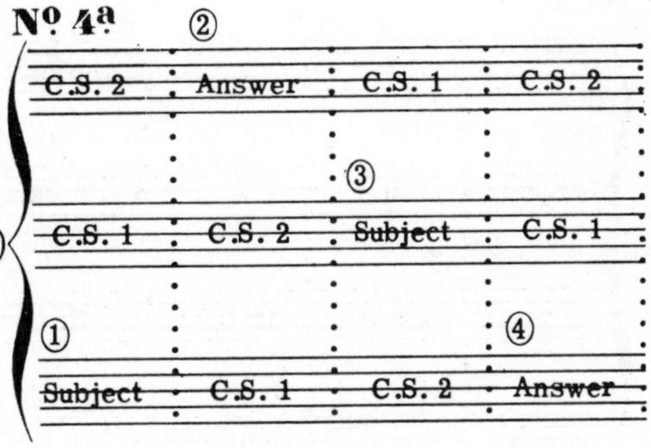

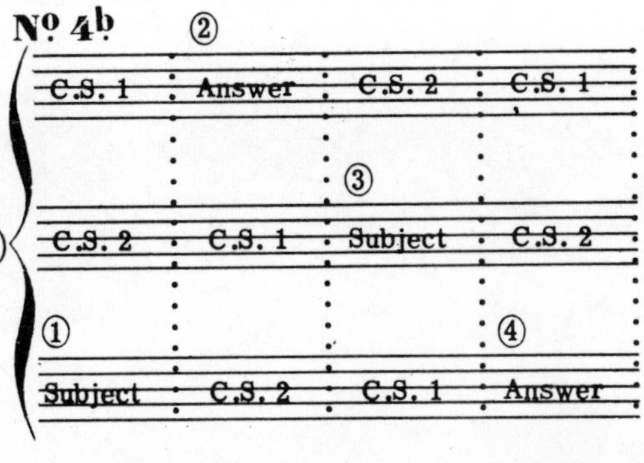

Same observation as for no. 1b.

151.

Exposition with Two Countersubjects (cont.)

2. In Four Parts

Nº 1.

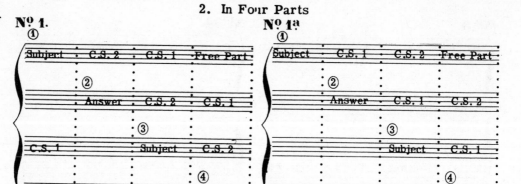

Nº 1ª

Nº 1ᵇ

Nº 2.   **Nº 2ª**

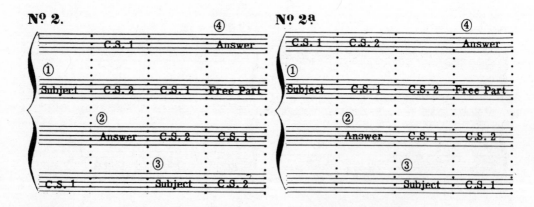

Nº 2ᵇ

Nᵒ 3.

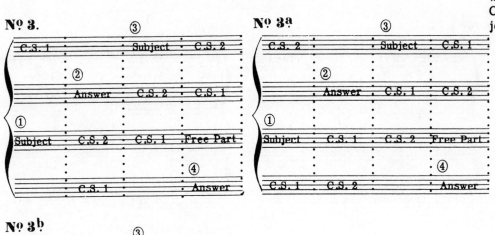

Nᵒ 3ᵃ

Nᵒ 3ᵇ

Nᵒ 4.

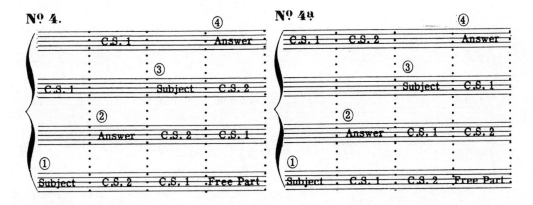

Nᵒ 4ᵃ

Nᵒ 4ᵇ

Exposition with Two Countersubjects (cont.)

152.   Dispositions to be used only in exceptional cases

Nº 1.

① Subject · C.S. 1 · C.S. 2 · Free Part
④
C.S. 1 · C.S. 2 · · Answer
③
C.S. 2 · · Subject · C.S. 1
②
· Answer · C.S. 1 · C.S. 2

Nº 1ª

① Subject · C.S. 2 · C.S. 1 · Free Part
④
C.S. 2 · C.S. 1 · · Answer
③
C.S. 1 · · Subject · C.S. 2
②
· Answer · C.S. 2 · C.S. 1

Nº 2.

② · Answer · C.S. 1 · C.S. 2
① Subject · C.S. 1 · C.S. 2 · Free Part
④
C.S. 1 · C.S. 2 · · Answer
③
C.S. 2 · · Subject · C.S. 1

Nº 2ª

② · Answer · C.S. 2 · C.S. 1
① Subject · C.S. 2 · C.S. 1 · Free Part
④
C.S. 2 · C.S. 1 · · Answer
③
C.S. 1 · · Subject · C.S. 2

Nº 3.

③ C.S. 2 · · Subject · C.S. 1
④
C.S. 1 · C.S. 2 · · Answer
① Subject · C.S. 1 · C.S. 2 · Free Part
②
· Answer · C.S. 1 · C.S. 2

Nº 3ª

③ C.S. 1 · · Subject · C.S. 2
④
C.S. 2 · C.S. 1 · · Answer
① Subject · C.S. 2 · C.S. 1 · Free Part
②
· Answer · C.S. 2 · C.S. 1

Nº 4.

② · Answer · C.S. 1 · C.S. 2
③
C.S. 2 · · Subject · C.S. 1
④
C.S. 1 · C.S. 2 · · Answer
① Subject · C.S. 1 · C.S. 2 · Free Part

Nº 4ª

② · Answer · C.S. 2 · C.S. 1
③
C.S. 1 · · Subject · C.S. 2
④
C.S. 2 · C.S. 1 · · Answer
① Subject · C.S. 2 · C.S. 1 · Free Part

153. **D.**

Models of expositions in which three countersubjects enter with the first entry of the subject.

No 1.

① Subj · CS 3 · CS 1 · CS 2
② CS 2 · Ans · CS 3 · CS 1
③ CS 1 · CS 2 · Subj · CS 3
④ CS 3 · CS 1 · CS 2 · Ans

No 1ª

① Subj · CS 2 · CS 3 · CS 1
② CS 1 · Ans · CS 2 · CS 3
③ CS 3 · CS 1 · Subj · CS 2
④ CS 2 · CS 3 · CS 1 · Ans

No 1ᵇ

① Subj · CS 1 · CS 2 · CS 3
② CS 3 · Ans · CS 1 · CS 2
③ CS 2 · CS 3 · Subj · CS 1
④ CS 1 · CS 2 · CS 3 · Ans

No 2.

④ CS 3 · CS 1 · CS 2 · Ans
① Subj · CS 3 · CS 1 · CS 2
② CS 2 · Ans · CS 3 · CS 1
③ CS 1 · CS 2 · Subj · CS 3

No 2ª

④ CS 1 · CS 2 · CS 3 · Ans
① Subj · CS 1 · CS 2 · CS 3
② CS 3 · Ans · CS 1 · CS 2
③ CS 2 · CS 3 · Subj · CS 1

No 2ᵇ

④ CS 2 · CS 3 · CS 1 · Ans
① Subj · CS 2 · CS 3 · CS 1
② CS 1 · Ans · CS 2 · CS 3
③ CS 3 · CS 1 · Subj · CS 2

No 3.

③ CS 1 · CS 2 · Subj · CS 3
② CS 2 · Ans · CS 3 · CS 1
① Subj · CS 3 · CS 1 · CS 2
④ CS 3 · CS 1 · CS 2 · Ans

No 3ª

③ CS 3 · CS 1 · Subj · CS 2
② CS 1 · Ans · CS 2 · CS 3
① Subj · CS 2 · CS 3 · CS 1
④ CS 2 · CS 3 · CS 1 · Ans

No 3ᵇ

③ CS 2 · CS 3 · Subj · CS 1
② CS 3 · Ans · CS 1 · CS 2
① Subj · CS 1 · CS 2 · CS 3
④ CS 1 · CS 2 · CS 3 · Ans

No 4.

④ CS 3 · CS 1 · CS 2 · Ans
③ CS 1 · CS 2 · Subj · CS 3
② CS 2 · Ans · CS 3 · CS 1
① Subj · CS 3 · CS 1 · CS 2

No 4ª

④ CS 2 · CS 3 · CS 1 · Ans
③ CS 3 · CS 1 · Subj · CS 2
② CS 1 · Ans · CS 2 · CS 3
① Subj · CS 2 · CS 3 · CS 1

No 4ᵇ

④ CS 1 · CS 2 · CS 3 · Ans
③ CS 2 · CS 3 · Subj · CS 1
② CS 3 · Ans · CS 1 · CS 2
① Subj · CS 1 · CS 2 · CS 3

**Expositions
with Three
Countersub-
jects (cont.)**

154.   Dispositions to be used only in exceptional cases.

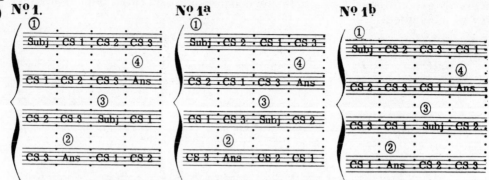

**Exposition
in Two
Parts.**

155. Exposition of a fugue in two parts (instrumental style)
Subject by A. Gedalge (for the answer to this subject see Sec. 75)

(a) Note that the codetta between the second and third entries is rather
extended. It is always thus in two-part fugues in which the second and third
entries are in the same voice (cf. illustration A, Sec. 142). The purpose of
this disposition is to set off better the return of the subject in the main key
and, at the same time, avoid the immediate repetition of the principal motif
of the fugue in the same voice.

156. Exposition of a vocal fugue in three parts with one countersubject.
Subject by A. Gedalge

Exposition in
Three Parts

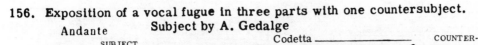

(a) The free part is based on the figure from the codetta,
in (b), (c), and (e) the figure is used in inversion,
in (d) it appears in direct motion.

157. Exposition on a subject which is calm and expressive, though it contains many notes.

Subject by E. Paladilhe

Andantino.

Exposition in
Four Parts

Subject
Announced in
the Soprano

In (a), (b) and (c), the fourth and sixth produced by the melodic movement of the subject should not be considered as a true six-four chord. It comes about from using the first degree as an auxiliary tone to the subdominant, and one should consider, in accordance with the rules of strict counterpoint, that the harmony is determined, not by the auxiliary tone, but by the subdominant.

(d) At the moment when the soprano is silent, the melodic line of the upper part is continued by the alto without interrupting in any way the flow of the melody in the upper voice.

The above observation is important. To maintain the melodic quality of a fugue, it is important that, if one part is interrupted, another part picks up the melodic line in such a way that the meaning of the musical discourse does not suddenly change. In short, all the parts, by their ensemble, must contribute to the melodic line of the fugue.

158. Exposition on a subject in vocal style, calm and expressive
Moderato.   Subject by Ambroise Thomas

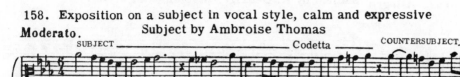

In (a), (b), and (c), note that the two free parts imitate each other. By means of such emphasis on a melodic figure in the exposition, one gains the right to use this figure in the development of the fugue.

(d) In certain schools of music, this attack of a major second (here between soprano and alto) is forbidden. As no one has ever given the reason for such a rule, I feel that, even in strict style, one may take this liberty (if it is a liberty) especially when the dissonant note (here the B-flat of the alto) has been used immediately before, an octave above or below, in one of the two parts of the forbidden dissonance.

159. Allegro Subject by A. Gedalge (instrumental style)

**Subject
Announced in
the Soprano**

(a) Note that the free part has been written so that it may be linked in a natural manner with the countersubject.

(b) The free parts are made of fragments of the countersubject and imitate each other.

160. Exposition on a subject in instrumental style. The use of a codetta has been avoided.

Subject by Reber

Subject
Announced in
the Soprano

161. In this exposition, a codetta could have been introduced after the first entry of the subject, to lead to the answer, and could have been written as follows:

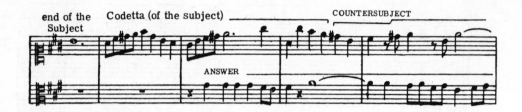

Here are the reasons which have led me to omit the codetta and to modulate immediately to the dominant key.

1. The subject ends with a bar devoid of rhythmic motion and melodic interest. Any codetta, then, seems foreign to the melody of the subject.

2. Because of the harmonies implied by the answer, no matter how the codetta is planned, it will use the same chords (B, A, E) that the countersubject must use. Thus there would be redundance and monotony.

That is why, in similar cases, it is better to modulate immediately to the dominant key instead of using a codetta.

162. Exposition on a fugue in instrumental style
            Subject by A. Gedalge

Subject Announced in the Soprano.

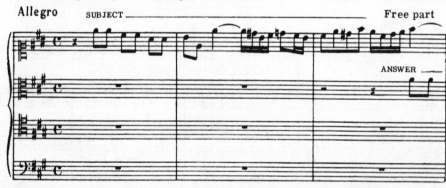

In this exposition, the rhythm and melody of the subject are not distorted by having the answer begin on the fourth beat when the subject begins on the second beat (Sec. 133).

In (a), the free part anticipates the rhythm of the countersubject to which it is linked without interruption.

In (b) and in the following bars, the free parts use fragments of the countersubject in imitation.

163. Exposition on a lively subject with a vivacious countersubject.

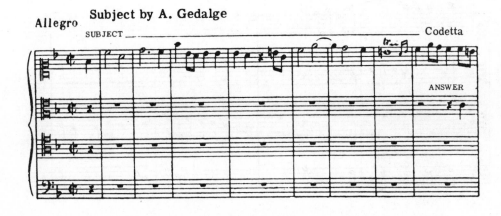

164. Exposition on a vocal subject of serious, sustained character

The free part (a) is imitated by the tenor in (c).

In (b) the alto attacks a seventh (B-flat) without preparation. This type of auxiliary, though certainly musical, is not always acceptable in examinations.

165. Exposition on a subject in instrumental style

**Subject
Announced in
the Alto.**

In (b) the two parts together combine to reproduce the melodic outlines of free part (a).

Beginning with the third entry, the two free parts continually present, in imitation, melodic and rhythmic designs that recall the rhythm of the first free part (a). Thus, they give the entire exposition a distinct melodic character and avoid dryness and lack of expressiveness — faults into which one could easily fall with such a subject.

166. Exposition on a calm, expressive subject. The parts use melodic figures containing many notes.

167. Exposition on a subject in vocal style, of calm character.
Subject by A. Gedalge

Subject Announced in the Tenor.

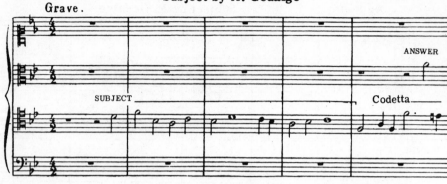

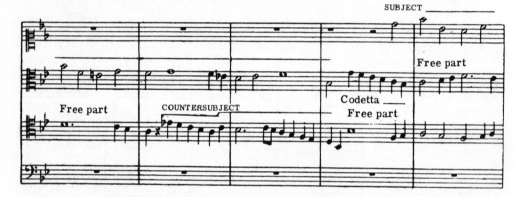

In (a) the ending of the countersubject has undergone a slight modification in order to avoid a perfect cadence on the first beat of the following bar. This practice is not always acceptable in the school fugue, though common practice among the masters.

168. Exposition on a calm, serious subject, with a countersubject some-what more flowing.

Subject by A. Gedalge

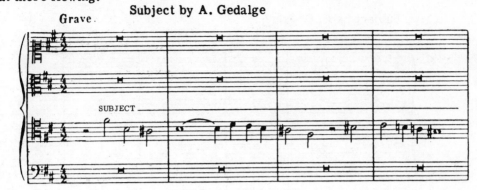

Subject
Announced in
the Tenor.

169. Exposition on a calm, serious subject, with a countersubject somewhat flowing and chromatic.

Subject by **A. Gedalge**

Moderato

**Subject
Announced in
the Bass.**

In (a) and (b) the augmented fifth on the first beat of the bar, produced by a contrary chromatic movement of the parts, is one of the most classic types. Its use is frequent among the masters of the fugue (cf. Bach, Mozart, Handel, etc.) who have always considered it an invertible interval.

170. Exposition on a calm, **expressive subject, in instrumental style**[1].

Subject by A. Gedalge

Moderato espressivo.

Subject
Announced in
the Bass.

1. On this subject and using this exposition, which I composed especially for her, Mlle. Josephine Boulay has written a very remarkable organ fugue (published by Durand et Fils, Paris).

171. Exposition on a subject of energetic character, with a vivacious countersubject and an extended codetta between the second and third entries. The codetta introduces a new figure which is in turn used in the free parts. (Instrumental style)   Subject by Onslow

Subject Announced in the Bass.

172. Exposition on a calm, expressive subject, the countersubject presented with the first entry of the subject. (Vocal style)

Subject by A. Gedalge

Andante espressivo

Countersubject Accompanying the First Entry of the Subject

N.B. At the École this D is considered forbidden, but it can be used outside the conservatories.

173. Exposition on a subject that is vivacious, but in a broad style. The countersubject accompanies the first entry of the subject.

Subject by Massenet

Countersubject Accompanying the First Entry of the Subject

174. Exposition of a fugue with one subject and two countersubjects accompanying the first entry of the subject.

Subject by Reber

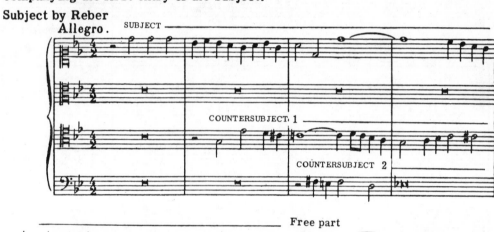

Two Countersubjects accompanying the First Entry of the Subject.

175. Exposition on a chromatic subject with two countersubjects introduced successively at the second and third entries. (For the answer to this subject, see Sections 92-98)

Subject by Cherubini

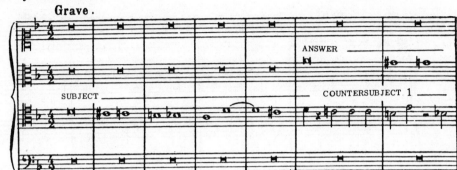

Two Countersubjects Introduced Successively

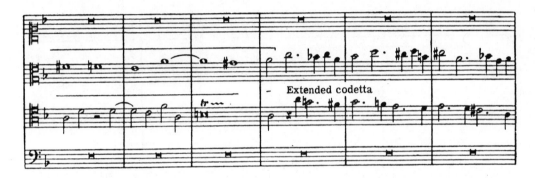

176. Exposition of a fugue with one subject and three countersubjects.

Subject by A. Gedalge

Maestoso.

Three Countersubjects Introduced with the First Entry of the Subject

In this fugue, note that a codetta has been introduced after each entry of the subject. That is always done in this type of fugue. Furthermore, it is necessary to introduce a rest in the part that is about to present the subject or answer.

Since every voice has, at all times, either the subject or one of the countersubjects, the codetta must be interpolated to make the entries stand out. It is also one of the faults of fugues with more than two countersubjects that they lack variety because of the necessity of constant repetition of the same melodic material.

CHAPTER VI

The Counter-Exposition

Definitions

177. The counter exposition is a second exposition which has only two entries.

It differs from the exposition in that the order of entries is the reverse of the order in the exposition. In the counter exposition the first entry is the answer and the second, the subject.

Furthermore, the answer must be introduced by one of the voices that had the subject in the exposition, and the subject appears in one of the parts that had the answer in the exposition.

178. The counter exposition is not required in a fugue. In addition, it can be used only when the tessitura of the subject lends itself to its appearance in one of the voices for which it was not originally composed. Such is not the case with most of the subjects that are given to students.

Generally speaking, a counter exposition is written only when the subject is very short; or when it lacks a sufficiently distinctive melodic character, so that four entries are not enough to impose it upon the attention of the listener.

Tonality

179. The counter exposition is always in the main key of the fugue.

It is separated from the exposition by a short episode.[1]

Placement of the Counter-subject.

180. Although it is obligatory in a counter exposition to have the answer and subject, respectively, enter in voices which had not had them in the exposition, one is free to place the countersubjects in any voice. The tessitura of the countersubject may determine its placement, or else one can proceed according to one's fancy.

181. Whenever a subject has more than four bars in moderate tempo, it is well to omit the counter exposition so as not to lengthen the fugue in an unnecessary manner.

182. The following illustrations show the various arrangements which can be adopted in a counter exposition for the successive entries of the answer and subject in two, three, or four parts.

1. See the following chapter on the subject of episodes.

Models of Counter Expositions

1. In Two Parts

2. In Three Parts
The countersubject entering after or at the same time as the subject

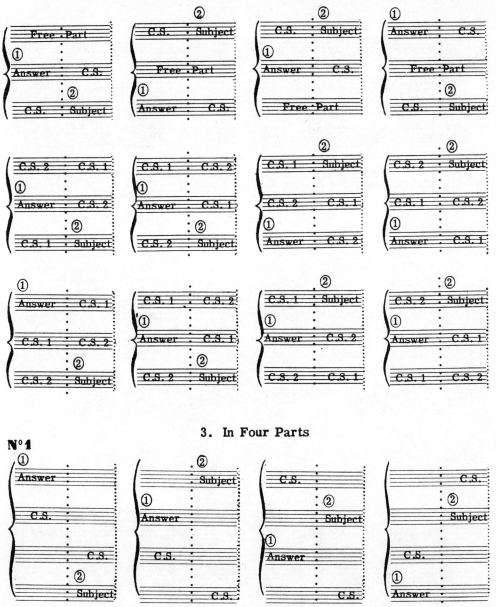

3. In Four Parts

The position of the countersubjects in a counter exposition of four parts is not fixed. It depends on the nature and range of these countersubjects and can be modified as the need arises.

183. Let us recall that, in a counter exposition, answer and subject must enter in voices other than those in which they entered in the exposition. We can, then, easily get a clear idea of the dispositions that should be used by comparing the illustrations on page 109 with those given in the preceding chapter.

184. For the sake of further clarification, here is an example of an exposition followed by an episode and a counter exposition.

Subject by Handel

(a) The treatment of this passage would be considered reprehensible at the École, although the clash of the three notes E, F, and G is very short-lived, especially in this rapid tempo.

(b) It is the same with the E of the bass in this bar. This note is a passing tone approached by a leap, as is forbidden in strict counterpoint. It should not be used in school examinations.

Note that, in the above counter exposition, the bass, which had the subject in the exposition, has the answer while the tenor has the entry of the subject.

The countersubjects are in the same order as in the exposition.

185. The counter exposition ends what is known as the first section of the fugue. It consists of:

> The exposition
> An episode
> The counter exposition

The First Section of the Fugue

If there is no counter exposition, the first section ends with the exposition. What follows constitutes the d e v e l o p m e n t of the fugue.

186. It is of the utmost importance for the student not to approach the study of the episode without knowing — and knowing well — how to compose an exposition. The exposition, in fact, is not only the most important part of the fugue from the viewpoint of the study of composition (since from it must come all the material of the fugue) but it is also the most difficult part to do successfully.

In the chapters that follow we shall consider the development of the fugue and the various devices used to give it variety in unity.

CHAPTER VII

The Fugal Episode

Definitions

187. In analyzing any musical phrase whatever, one is quickly made aware that it has a certain symmetry which results from the repetition of the same melodic or rhythmic ideas at various intervals and various distances.

This more or less frequent repetition of similar fragments necessarily brings about a series of harmonic progressions of the same type. Thus a harmonic sequence is produced, one that is more or less regular and more or less complex.

188. The episode of a fugue consists precisely of a series of imitations which are more or less close and are formed of fragments of the subject, countersubject, codetta, or free parts of the exposition combined so that their whole forms an uninterrupted melodic line and leads in a natural way to the re-entries of the subject and answer in keys related to the main key of the subject.

The keys to which the school fugue modulates are, for each mode, the five whose signature differs from that of the main key only by a sharp or flat more or less, and the relative major or minor mode, as the case may be.[1]

189. If one takes a very short melodic idea and systematically transposes it to different pitches, the harmonic progressions of the first presentation will be regularly reproduced at each repetition of the original idea; and a harmonic sequence will inevitably come about.

190. From the above definitions it can be seen that:

1. The episodes of a fugue are based on more or less regular harmonic sequences.
2. The main motive of an episode must be derived from the subject, countersubject, codetta, or one of the free parts of the exposition.
3. It should be exclusively melodic.

The harmonic progression which serves as a basis should no more be visible than the framework of a house after it is built.

---

1. See Sections 344-345 for the order in which these different tonalities occur.

191. At the École, harmonic sequences in the fugue are strictly forbidden. **The Use of**
This is all very well if one understands by it that, in episodes, one should **Harmonic**
not have simple progressions of chords, whether ornamented or not. To take **Sequences.**
a simple harmonic structure, such as is found in harmony exercises, and repeat it at different pitch levels, offers nothing of musical interest.

But this rule is not good if one is trying to construct an episode without
basing it on one or more harmonic progressions, simple or complex. It is
only necessary to analyze any musical work to be convinced that the chord
progressions, based on patterns that are more or less regular, are the basis
itself, the substratum of all development.

192. The quality of an episode depends on: **Quality of**
    1. The choice of motive or theme upon which it is based. **the Episode.**
    2. The melodic line constructed with this motive by the com-
       poser.
    3. The work of realization, which consists of applying to the
       motive of the episode all the devices of fugue style.

193. The main motive of an episode, as we have said, can be taken only **Main Motive**
from one of the figures used in the exposition of the fugue (subject, countersub- **of the**
ject, codetta, free parts). **Episode.**

One may base an episode on a simple rhythmic or melodic figure composed of only a few notes, or on a melodic idea that is rather long. One may
also build the episode on two, three, or four motives taken from the exposition and combined in simple or invertible counterpoint.

194. The melodic structure of the line using the elements of the episode
depends greatly upon the imagination of the musician. In this respect, one
can only advise close attention to, and exhaustive study of, the works of Bach,
Mozart, and Mendelssohn.

195. So as not to be bewildered by the problem of choosing motives for **Preparation**
episodes, the student should restrict himself to the following procedure. Once **of the**
the exposition of the fugue is finished, he extracts from it, carefully, all the **Episode.**
melodic or rhythmic figures which can give rise to imitations or other contrapuntal combinations:
    1. in direct motion, with or without   ⎫
    2. in inversion, with or without   ⎪ augmentation
    3. in simple retrograde, with or without ⎬   or
    4. in simple retrograde and retrograde ⎪ diminution
       inversion combined, with or without ⎭
These devices should be familiar to students who have studied counterpoint.

**Exposition
Analyzed
from the
Point of View
of Episodes.**

196. Let us take as an example the following exposition from the Well-Tempered Clavier, II, Fugue No. 8 of J. S. Bach.

Here is a detailed analysis of this exposition.

197. Considering the subject alone, we can divide it into fragments or melodic motives.

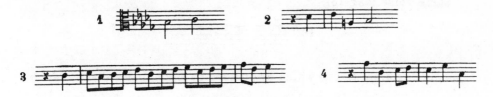

Looking at it in inversion, we have the following material:

198. The countersubject, analyzed in turn, will supply us with the following elements, the first two of which may be thought of as variants of a single chromatic motive:

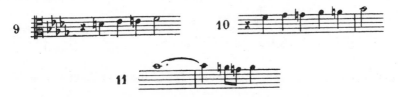

and respectively, in inversion:

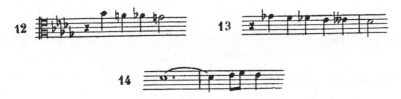

One could use only one fragment of a figure, for example

(11ᵃ) ...   or (14ᵃ) ...

or else:

(11ᵇ) ...   (14ᵇ) ...

199. From the free parts we can cull the following fragments:

(Exposition, bar 11, soprano):

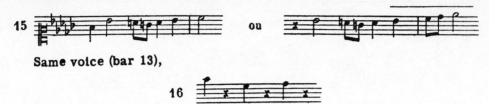

Same voice (bar 13),

a purely rhythmic figure which is utilised by Bach under diverse forms:

Bach uses it, in the course of the fugue, only for rhythmic imitations.
One should also consider these various fragments in inversion.

In bars 14 and 15 we again find, in the soprano, two figures very similar in rhythm and included in the same melodic fragment.

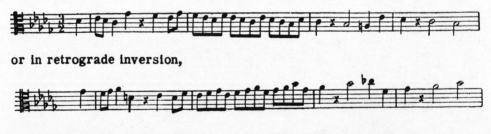

They are both derived, moreover, from the free part in bar 11.

200. The same thing can be done to the subject taken in retrograde:

or in retrograde inversion,

as well as to the countersubject and the free parts, in retrograde and retrograde inversion.

201. For the subject given here, augmentation or diminution are out of the question, since subjects in ternary meter usually do not lend themselves to this type of treatment.

In this fugue, however, Bach used once only a fragment of his countersubject in augmentation and inversion combined.

It is a good idea to call to the attention of students that the possibilities of augmentation and diminution should never be neglected in their preliminary consideration of subjects to be worked with, for they are frequently used, and to very good advantage.

We shall come back to this matter later on (Sections 251-254).

202. When the student has thus assembled all the elements which he might use for the development of the fugue, he should select several and combine them to outline the melodic line of each episode.

We have already pointed out above that this melodic line should always be based upon one or upon a series of harmonic sequences.

Let us take, from a random subject,

Construction
of the
Melodic Line
of the
Episode

one of the figures from which it has been formed, and let us give it a logical harmonic bass:

203. It is quite obvious that we could set aside the upper part and use this bass to create all kinds of harmonic sequences at whatever pitches we transposed the bass to. It is no less obvious that each time this bass is used, we will be able to superimpose upon it, at the corresponding pitch level, the melodic figure which gave rise to it.

204. If, in addition, we know beforehand the tonality we should like to have the passage end in, we have only to arrange it in such a way as to modulate to the desired key over a more or less related tonal path.

Suppose, for example, we should like to modulate to the key of B-flat minor. We might then arrange our sequence as follows:

Should we desire a longer progression modulating, for example, to D-flat (the fifth degree of the main key) we might arrange our sequence this way:

205. But as it is, this passage will never be anything but a harmonic sequence treated melodically. The melodic figure should therefore be used successively in different voices (imitations).

Example:

206. With the outline of the episode thus established and the imitations prepared, we must remember that we cannot use the other voices as simple harmonic fill-ins. On the contrary, the other parts must of necessity be treated melodically in simple or double counterpoint, and all the melodic figures must come from the subject, countersubject, or other part of the exposition.

We therefore have to choose and prepare the materials that can be combined before we go further.

207. Since, in the case at hand, there is no exposition, we shall simply utilize the fragment given:

It may be considered in the three following ways:

1. In its totality

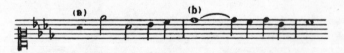

2. As having in the first bar (a) a melodic figure:

that can be used in double counterpoint with the second bar;

3. As having in the second bar (b) a melodic figure likewise invertible:

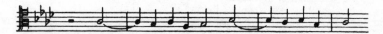

Then, in order to avoid the monotony resulting from a descending line, we can end with an ascending line (D) built on the last fragment (b) given above:

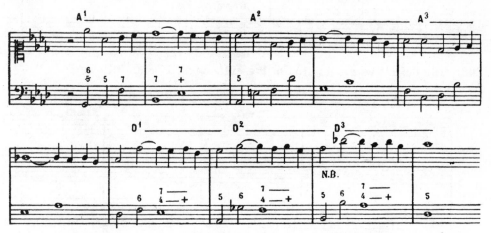

N.B. Note that, in the next to the last bar, the sequence ceases to be regular and ascends one extra degree.

208. With this preliminary work completed, and having before us the various combinations of the given fragment that can be inverted in triple counterpoint,

we can now make a plan of execution for the whole episode:

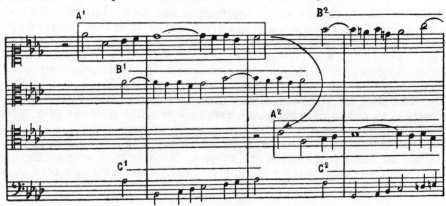

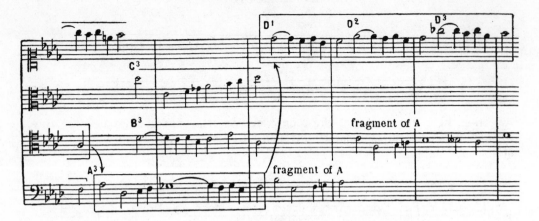

209. The definitive realisation of the episode will be as follows:

210. One can study the above realization and appreciate the difference between it and the harmonic sequence from which it arose. Nevertheless, upon hearing it, one gets a feeling, a clear impression of this underlying harmony. Through the varied arrangement of the parts, however, the dryness and monotony of a simple chord progression, inevitable with even a slight prolongation, has been avoided.

It will be seen later, however, that there are cases in which the use of an apparently pure and simple harmonic sequence is quite effective (Sec. 216).

Episode on Several Motives.

211. All the elements in the episode which we have just studied have been taken from the same fragment of the subject. With them, one may also combine various figures taken from the subject, countersubject, or a free part of the exposition.

In this case, in planning the episode, one selects for the main motive either the longest melodic figure, or the one with the most outstanding rhythmic or melodic character. The other motives serve, in a sense, as countersubjects.

212. These various motives are used, at the will of the composer, in simple, double, triple, or quadruple counterpoint, depending upon their number.

The imitative combinations in which they are used may be free or strict, successive or canonic, direct, inverted, or retrograde; or they may be in augmentation or diminution, etc.

213. In any case, the main motive of an episode, considered as the antecedent of the harmonic sequence, the basis of the episode, should remain within a single tonality. That is, it should end with a cadence in the same key in which it begins. Later on we shall see that, in the realization of the episode, the cadence is always avoided by means of one of the devices customary in musical composition.

> Main Motive of an Episode does not Modulate.

The modulations required by the harmonic scheme will be brought about either by means of notes common to the last chord of the antecedent and the first chord of the consequent, or by means of a modulating coda. It can be easily understood that if the initial presentation of the pattern modulates, this modulation may well cause the episode to go around the circle of keys.

214. Invention, in an episode, comes more from the character of the motives than from their arrangement.

This observation arises from a comparison of fugues written by the masters of all schools. In their fugues, the episodes, whose variety seems considerable at first sight, are all derived from a rather limited number of basic combinations, which the student should become very familiar with.

These rather fundamental arrangements result from the application of the rules relating to the different kinds of imitation. Moreover, they can be varied almost indefinitely in their combination and their reciprocal penetration.

215. We have seen above that, after the motives of the episode were chosen and harmonized, and the melodic line constructed, the imitations were arranged in a way that would make the entries stand out.

These arrangements can be summed up in the six kinds of combinations described below:

> Disposition of Imitations in an Episode.

216. CASE I. EACH PART HAS ITS OWN SEPARATE FIGURE

Each part imitates itself by repeating, at different pitch levels, the figure which is given to it in the antecedent.

> A Separate Figure in Each Part.

This is the procedure of the pure and simple harmonic sequence. It can be used in a fugue only on the condition that it be extremely musical. In such a case, the episode should be based on melodically interesting motives, or ones that are not too long.

Nevertheless, this type of combination is frequently used at the end of one of the other types of episodes. It has the advantage of preparing the re-entry of the subject in a rather animated way, and, in this case, the fragment which serves as its main motive should be very short. We shall give examples later on.

An example of an episode in which the material of the antecedent is repeated in the same voice with each recurrence:

Elements of the Episode

Bach WTC I, Fugue 18

c) **Episode from J. S. Bach's organ fugue in F minor**

The main motive and melodic line are in the upper part

Subject in the dominant _____ etc

217. CASE II. ALL PARTS ARE DERIVED FROM THE MAIN MOTIVE.

Main Motive in a Single Part.

The main motive stays in one of the parts, which has the melodic line of the episode. The other parts have fragments of the main motive, either in imitation or repetition at various pitch levels. This procedure, which is related to the preceding one in that it leaves the harmonic framework exposed, differs from it in that all its parts are derived from the main motive. Thus, canonic imitation is possible. Although it is difficult to handle in an interesting way, this type of episode offers the advantage of lending itself to all kinds of close imitations.

In this connection, J.S. Bach's organ fugue on the following subject

may be studied with profit, for nearly all its episodes are constructed in the above manner. Examples:

218. a) End of the exposition   Canonic imitation of the main motive

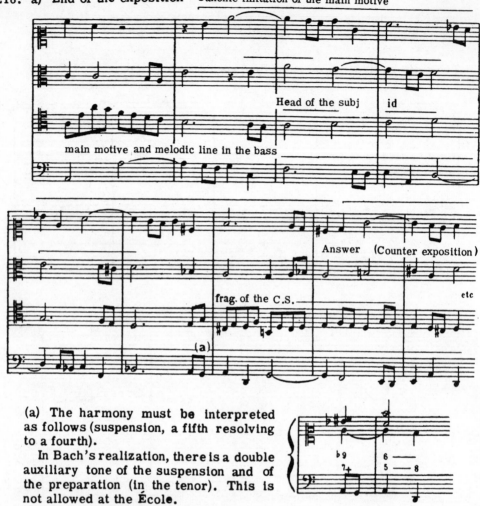

(a) The harmony must be interpreted as follows (suspension, a fifth resolving to a fourth).

In Bach's realization, there is a double auxiliary tone of the suspension and of the preparation (in the tenor). This is not allowed at the École.

219. b) Episode on the same motive, but more condensed, and with canonic imitation in three parts:

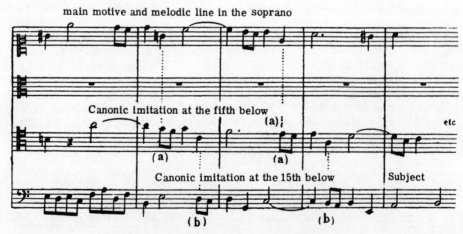

(a) Direct unisons are forbidden at the École, as well as the auxiliary at the unison.

(b) At the École, it is not permitted to use as an auxiliary in the lower part a note used in another part.

220. c) Main motive and melodic line in the upper part (Bach, Well-Tempered Clavier, II, Fugue 22 in B-flat minor, whose exposition has been analyzed above):

Elements of the Episode

(A) Combination of the two elements to form the main motive

Melodic and harmonic plan

Realisation of J.S.Bach

221. d) J. S. Bach, Well-Tempered Clavier, I, Fugue 12.

222. e) J. S. Bach, Organ Fugue:

b) **Realisation by Bach**

main motive and melodic line in the bass

a ————————

Subject in inversion

etc.

Coda

223. Note, in this episode, with what skill Bach has avoided the coldness and dryness which would have been produced by absolute symmetry of all the parts if the imitations had occurred regularly in each voice on the same beat. With his ingenious handling of the parts, he could, with the same rhythmic figure, create a canonic imitation between soprano and tenor and handle it so that, while the bass is ascending, the ensemble of the three upper parts descends.

224. Here, from the same fugue, is an episode in five parts in which the melodic line remains in the upper part while the bass has a free rhythmic imitation in augmentation and inversion of a fragment of the subject. The other parts imitate each other by continually repeating at different pitch levels the same melodic and rhythmic figure. Note that, since the majority of the examples cited below are taken from instrumental fugues, they generally exceed the ranges of vocal composition, as must not be done in the school fugue, which always is considered vocal.

a) main motive

Elements of the Episode

b) Rhythmic imitation in inversion and augmentation

**Main Motive
in Two Parts.**

225. CASE III. TWO PARTS IMITATE EACH OTHER, USING THE SAME MOTIVE ALTERNATELY:

The main melodic line of the episode alternates between the same two parts. The other parts imitate each other, using either fragments of the main motive or various figures taken from the subject, countersubject, or from the free parts of the exposition.

a) The following example is taken from the Bach fugue in B-flat minor previously discussed (Well-Tempered Clavier, II, 22). The numbers placed above the melodic figures of the episode refer to the analysis of the exposition of this fugue on pages 114-115.

Elements of the Episode

a) Melodic and harmonic plan of the episode

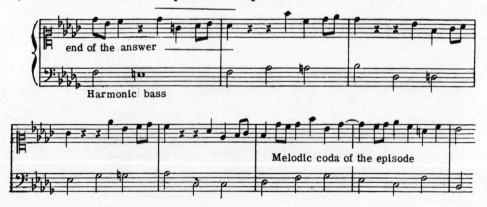

b) Plan of execution

c) Realisation of Bach

226. b) **Episode in three parts (two parts in canon).** (J. S. Bach, Well-Tempered Clavier, II, Fugue 7).

**Main Motive
in Imitation
in Two Parts**

227. **CASE IV. THE PARTS IMITATE EACH OTHER TWO BY TWO.**

The main motive of the episode is accompanied by a second figure which serves as a sort of countersubject. The melodic line remains constantly in the same part, or, more rarely, the two groups of voices alternate and have, by turns, the main motive and its countersubject.

Examples:

a) **Mozart, Sonata in A for Violin and Piano, K. 402 (385e). Fugue finale**

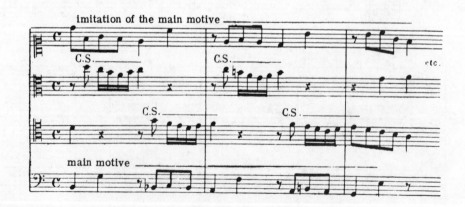

b) Mozart, Quartet in A Major, K. 464. Third Movement.

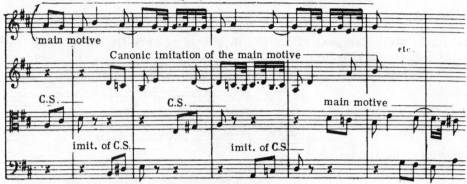

c) Bach, The Art of Fugue, Contrapunctus IV.

d) Ibid. Another episode on the same motive, with a different disposition of parts.

This type of episode is rarely used alone. It tends to be rather dry. It is generally found combined with one or more of the other arrangements analyzed here, or else it is used for only very short episodes.

228. CASE V. THE MAIN MOTIVE OF THE EPISODE IS IMITATED IN THREE PARTS.

Main Motive in Three Parts.

The main melodic line of the episode passes through three parts. The fourth part can imitate itself by continually repeating the same figure, or it can borrow from the other parts figures which they use when they do not have the main motive, or else it can be composed of various figures taken from the subject, countersubject, or free parts of the exposition.

Example:

a) Bach, Well-Tempered Clavier, II, Fugue 22 in B-flat Minor (see the exposition, Sections 196-200).

229. The preceding episode approaches the canonic episode in its structure. It does not, however, have the strictness of the canon. In reality one
can see that, though the three motives or figures which form it continually
overlap each other and are, for the most part, written in triple counterpoint,
the overlapping does not always occur in the same voice, as it would if the
canon were regular. In a canon, the figures should follow each other in every
part in an invariable order, for example (A) (C) (B) or (A) (B) (C), etc.

230. Bach, Well-Tempered Clavier, I, Fugue 4 (in five parts).

231. CASE VI. THE FOUR PARTS IMITATE EACH OTHER.

Main Motive
in Four Parts

The melodic line of the episode passes successively through the four
parts which, one after the other, have the main motive.

This type of episode provides a greater richness and a greater variety
than the preceding ones. It lends itself to every type of imitation. The main
motive can be combined with a second or third motive or countersubject
written in invertible counterpoint. The disposition of the episode then recalls
that of the exposition with each motive appearing alternately in each part —
with this difference, however, that, in the episode, the imitations of the motives are at arbitrarily selected intervals.

Examples:
a) Bach, Well-Tempered Clavier, I, Fugue 24

Episode
on a single motive

232. b) Handel, Utrecht Jubilate

233. c) J. S. Bach, Organ Fugue in E-flat

234. The following episodes are canonic. By comparing them to the preceding ones, one can see the increased interest that canonic composition brings to the episode.

For the record, we shall later give a clear description of how to write an episode that is completely canonic. Although students who study fugue are already familiar with the various kinds of imitation, we have thought in the present case that it was a good idea to recall the structure of the invertible canon, in order to make use of it in an episode.

Canonic Episode.

The example which we shall analyze is in six parts, but the canon has only four. The method, in any case, is the same for a smaller or larger number of parts.

The canonic form should be preferred, for it allows the episode a tighter structure and a greater melodic richness.

a) Fugue on the Chorale "Jesus Christus, unser Heiland"— J. S. Bach

Realisation
of J.S. Bach

235. b) J. S. Bach, Well-Tempered Clavier, II, Fugue 9
Canonic episode on a fragment of the countersubject

Subject

236. Here is another episode in six parts by J. S. Bach, taken from the Construction
fugue ''ricercata'' of the Musical Offering. The subject is as follows: of the Canonic
Episode.

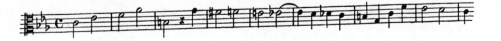

This episode is built entirely on the four following figures in accordance with the method used in canonic composition: that is, the parts are constructed in such a way that each one will produce with the others a self-sufficient harmony that may or may not be invertible, as required.

The figures are then linked together in such an order and at such intervals that, in their combination, they produce a continuous melodic line which is the main melodic line of the episode.

Then, with one of these figures (or two if they are invertible, as is the present case) the harmonic plan of the episode is laid out.

N.B. In its final term, the sequence ceases to be regular.

237. One can easily see that, once the parts have been combined in this way beforehand, each fragment can be used with the others at a pitch level

determined by the entry of the figure which has been selected for the head of the main motive.

One may then arrange the parts as one wishes, and the realisation takes place quite naturally. If the realisation has more than four parts, one may, when a voice has completed its entry of the main motive, either terminate it or give it other free imitations.

If the original plan is not invertible, the figures which make it up can appear only in their original harmonic disposition. To make it possible to change this arrangement, the parts must be written in double, triple, or quadruple counterpoint, according to their number.

238. Here is Bach's realisation:

239. Note that several times in this example the various fragments which make up the main motive have undergone modifications necessitated by the ranges of the voices or by the disposition of the parts. It is always permissible to do this whenever a better ensemble sound or a better musical effect can be obtained. One is limited only by the obligation not to distort the figures to the extent that they become unrecognizable. In any case the musical effect should never be sacrificed to a contrapuntal combination no matter how ingenious it might be.

Résumé

240. Summing up all the examples given above, it can be seen that the disposition of the parts in an episode is always the result of one of the following procedures (the choice will be determined by the character of the motives and by the effect desired):

1. Each part imitates itself (repeats its own melodic element at various pitch levels);
2. Two parts imitate each other, the others imitate themselves;
3. The parts imitate each other two by two;
4. Three parts imitate each other;
5. All the parts imitate each other.

241. Although there is often found in the works of the masters an entire episode based upon the exclusive use of one of the above procedures, in such cases the episode is rather short. In the modern fugue, in which more extended episodes are customary, it is well not to construct them on one formula but to combine several different procedures. Bach's fugues, as well as those of Mendelssohn and Mozart, furnish numerous examples of such combinations.

Episode on Successive Themes

242. Furthermore, an extended episode may be begun with one or more figures taken from the exposition of the fugue and may be continued with other elements (always taken, of course, from the same source). In such cases,

however, care should be taken that the different motives which succeed each
other are handled with enough skill so that there is no interruption in the
melodic line, and so that the motives succeed each other in a natural manner.

The examples cited below substantiate what we have set forth, and we
strongly advise students to analyze, in a similar manner, the largest possible
number of episodes from the fugues of the masters.

243. The example which follows is taken from the organ fugue in G major
by J. S. Bach. Here is its subject:

J.S.BACH.

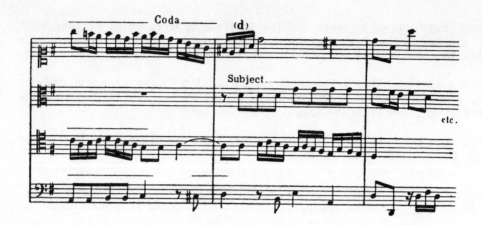

244. In this episode, from (a) to (b) the melodic line, based on the main motive,

alternates between the soprano and alto, the parts imitating each other two by two.

Beginning with (b), the main motive of the episode changes and, until the re-entry of the subject at (d), the main melodic line remains entirely in the soprano voice, with two different dispositions, however. From (b) to (c), each part, except the soprano, has a series of rather irregular imitations. The bass and alto have imitations of rhythm while the tenor imitates fragments of the main melodic line.

Beginning with (c), the episode is written in three parts only. There is a canon between soprano and tenor, and the bass imitates itself.

245. Here is an example by Mendelssohn (fugue for organ, op. 37, no. 1)

Mendelssohn, Fugue for Organ, op. 37, no. 1.

This episode is based on four figures. The first, introduced in the tenor, uses the head of the subject:

This figure constitutes the main motive and gives the episode its main melodic line.

The second figure, introduced at the beginning of the episode in the soprano part, is imitated in the bass in inversion (fourth bar and beginning of the fifth).

The third motive is used in imitation between soprano and bass.

Finally, the fourth, introduced in the middle of the second bar in the tenor, appears in the third bar in the alto.

In the ensemble, from (a) to (b) the parts imitate each other in two's, and from (b) to (c), that is, up to the re-entry of the subject at the fourth degree, each part imitates itself. Note that in this last part of the episode, the imitations of motives II and III are purely rhythmic, for these motives are substantially deformed here. This is a license permitted even in the most rigorous school fugue, in which entire episodes are often composed of purely rhythmic imitations.

246. We shall give several more examples without analyzing them, however. We shall leave this task to the student, who may be guided in this work by the preceding analyses. Furthermore, he will find abundant material for similar studies in the preludes and fugues of Bach and Mendelssohn and in a number of quartets and symphonies of Haydn, Mozart, and Beethoven. In these latter he should take note of the practical application to musical development of the devices employed in the fugue. We shall return later, and in a very special way, to this last point of view which is, basically, the main purpose of an extensive study of fugue.

a) J. S. Bach, Well-Tempered Clavier, II, Fugue 17

N.B. At the École, it is forbidden for parts to enter on appoggiaturas, as at (a) and (b).

b) **J. S. Bach, Prelude for Organ in C minor**

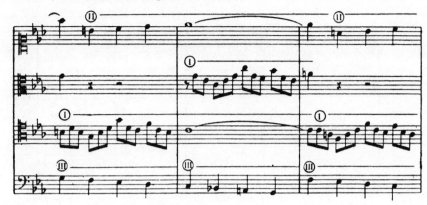

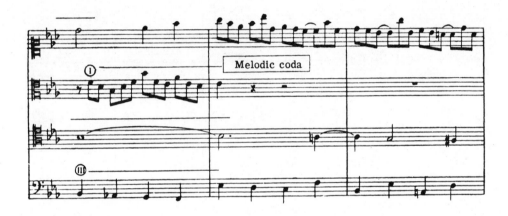

Although this episode is not taken from a fugue, it offers such a characteristic example of method that I cannot leave it unmentioned. The melodic coda which ends it is more extended than is customary in the school fugue. It should be noted, however, that this type of coda finds logical application in every type of fugue at the end of a spirited or expressive episode and contributes to making the entry of the subject in a new key stand out.

c) R. Schumann, Fugue No. 3 on the Name of Bach

In this example, the entries of the various motives are not emphasized enough. The whole is slightly thick and heavy and stems rather from a harmony exercise than from fugal composition. This episode must therefore be considered not as a model of composition but rather as one of melodic structure and line. Like the preceding one, this episode ends with a coda that brings back the subject at the cadence. The coda in the Bach example, however, is clearly melodic, and here it has a harmonic character, with the parts moving note against note in a quite characteristically chordal manner.

d) Mozart, Quartet in A major, K. 464

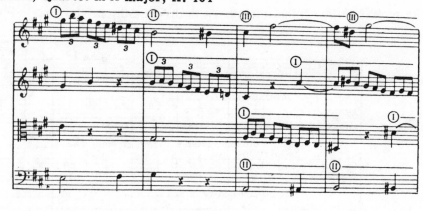

247. We have noted that all the figures in an episode may be imitated in inversion. This type of imitation is often employed with the dispositions previously studied.

Use of Inversion

Inversion may be used in the episode against direct motion, as in the following examples:

a) Mendelssohn, Organ Fugue, op. 37, no. 3
Here is the main motive of the episode:

its inversion is as follows:

One can consider this as the melodic plan of the episode:

In the realisation, the parts imitate each other by two's, the ones using

the motive in inversion, the others in direct motion.

b) André Gedalge, Four Preludes and Fugue for Piano, No. 2[1]

1. Ricordi, Paris.

248. In other cases, all the elements of the episode are in inversion.

This arrangement is less frequently employed, for, not having the advantage of contrast between the two, it also offers less of interest. There are, however, several examples in Bach in which the motive in inversion has enough relief to serve as the basis of the episode.

The following example comes from the fugue in B-flat minor cited above (Bach, Well-Tempered Clavier, II, 22). Here all the figures are in inversion, the main motive of the episode as well as the subsidiary motives. The figures which were used to construct this episode were analyzed in Sec. 197.

Reentry of the Subject in inversion

249. Retrograde and retrograde inversion are less frequently used in the fugue. Actually, all subjects do not lend themselves to this treatment, either because of their rhythmic structure or because, taken in retrograde, they lose all musical character.

However, whenever a subject can be utilized in this form, there may be material for episodes or interesting combinations. Example:

Retrograde and Retrograde Inversion Combined.

André Gedalge,[1] Four Preludes and Fugues for Piano, No. 3

a) **Direct motion combined with simple retrograde (episode with canon between two parts).**

b) **Direct motion combined with retrograde and retrograde inversion (the three parts in canon).**

1. Ricordi, Paris.

250. There is an observation to be made with respect to the two preceding episodes: Note that they have as their main motive the entire subject. This practice is frequent in the free fugue when the subject is short and the tempo, rapid. In the school fugue, however, where the subjects are generally more extended, this method is not employed.

251. Employment of augmentation in episodes is rather rare. As we shall see later on, this device is found much more often in the stretto, where it can be employed with telling effect.   **Augmentation.**

The following example (a), in six parts, comes from a fugue already cited, in Bach's Musical Offering. The upper part has, in augmentation, a figure used in imitation by the second soprano and alto, and afterwards by the bass.

The second example is taken from Bach's Well-Tempered Clavier, Book I, Fugue 7.

Diminution. 252. Diminution is more often used in the episodes which come between the exposition and the stretto. Diminution, as opposed to augmentation, has the effect of contracting the figures to which it is applied and allowing closer entries.

Augmentation is more appropriate in the stretto, for, when it is applied to the subject, it affords an opportunity for presenting subject and answer several times and simultaneously in different voices while one voice carries the subject in augmentation.

The use of diminution negates **an absurd** rule stated in several textbooks on fugue which forbids the occurrence in any part of **the fugue** of note values shorter than those found in the subject.

Augmentation and Diminution with Retrograde and Retrograde Inversion. 253. The main motive of the episode in augmentation or diminution can, at the same time, appear in inversion, retrograde, or retrograde inversion.

The following example illustrates one of those combinations where the motive in diminution occurs in the same passage in both direct motion and inversion.

Mozart,　Two Fantasies and Fugues for Piano, Four Hands　(No. 2)

Double Augmentation and Double Diminution. 254. Finally, we must mention episodes based on imitation in double augmentation or double diminution. Examples are most apt to be found in fugues written on chorale melodies, where the use of such devices arises naturally from the character of the fugues themselves.

The example which follows can be considered to be either simple or double augmentation or diminution, depending upon whether fragment (a), (b), or (c) is taken as the main motive.

Example:

J.S.BACH: "Ach Gott und Herr"

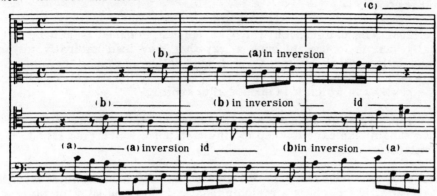

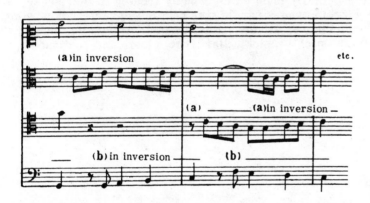

255. We have now completed the technical study of the episode. The student should become familiar with the various types discussed above. Later, when we discuss the musical composition of the fugue, we shall point out to him the considerations that may guide him in the choice of motives for the episodes, and in what order these motives should preferably be presented; in a word, just how he should go about it so that the mechanics will not be obvious to the listener. The better he has assimilated the technical part of the fugue, the better will he be master of his pen, the less the workmanship will show through, and the freer his imagination will be. With a minimum of effort, the result will be better.

256. There remain several conclusions to be drawn from the examples cited above. You have noticed how frequent the entries of voices are in all the passages cited. That is because the parts (and this is of the greatest importance) are not always used all at the same time. Entries must be preceded by rests. As a result, the episodes in a four-part fugue are more often written in three parts than in four.

Conclusions

257. Entries should always be made on figures taken from the subject, countersubject, or free parts of the exposition. They should never be made simply to fill out the harmony.

A voice should never drop out without reason. If it drops out, it is necessary that, taken by itself, it should imply a cadential harmony, perfect or otherwise.

258. The patterns on which an episode is based should be set up logically, that is to say, in such a way that they lead naturally to the desired modulation, either by means of a modulating sequence, or, not modulating, one which ends with a modulation necessary to the re-entry of the subject in the new key in which it is supposed to appear.

259. When an episode is constructed on two or more different patterns, one should take care to keep for the last those which give rise to the closest imitations.

260. It is necessary, in order to sustain the musical interest of the fugue, to treat all the parts in a melodic fashion in keeping with the style of the subject. The top voice especially must be rigorously treated in this sense, and the bass under no circumstances should take on the character of a simple harmonic bass. Furthermore, all the parts, in their ensemble, must unite in creating the impression of a melodic line, free, clear, and continuous.

CHAPTER VIII

The Stretto[1]

Definitions

261. In the exposition, entries of subject and answer follow each other in an invariable manner, the one appearing only after the other ends. If, by some device, the answer enters before the subject has finished its entry, a stretto occurs.

262. The word stretto (past participle of the Italian verb stringere, to squeeze) is therefore applied to any combination in which the entry of the answer is made at a closer distance from the head of the subject than in the exposition.

263. By extension, stretto designates the whole of the last section of the fugue, in which all the entries of the answer become closer and closer to the head of the subject.

264. As corollary to the preceding definitions, it may be said that:
1. The head of the subject and of the answer are the indispensable elements of a stretto, to the exclusion of any other figure in the subject.
Therefore,
2. A stretto can be composed of successive and constricted entries of only the head of the subject and of the answer.

265. By extension, however, one also calls strettos the close entries of the head of the countersubject of the subject and the head of the countersubject of the answer.

266. Four cases may present themselves in a stretto:
Case I. The theme of the subject can be continued in its entirety while the answer has its entry.
This is called a canonic stretto.

Canonic Stretto

Example:

---

1. See Editor's Introduction

267. This combination can occur with any number of parts.

Example:

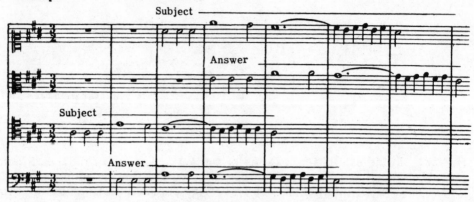

Disposition of the Voices

268. The order in which the voices enter is in no way fixed and depends solely upon the wish of the composer, on harmonic requirements, or upon the sonority desired. The preceding stretto could just as well be presented in this form:

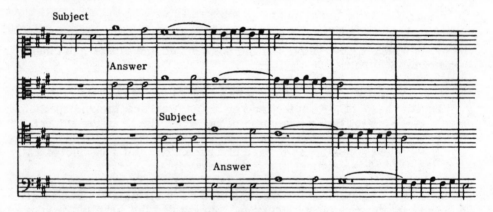

Entries on Unisons

269. The following disposition is not as good because the last entries come on unisons which should be avoided:

Here, the unisons prevent a clear perception of each entry and harm the effectiveness of their closeness.

270. A stretto also exists when a close canonic entry begins with the answer.

Example:

This is what is called a reversed canonic stretto. This type of stretto can be applied to any number of parts in the same way as the preceding one.

271. Case II. The theme of the subject cannot be continued in its entirety upon the close entry of the answer.

In such a case it is either modified towards its end, or else it is interrupted to be replaced by another figure. It should, however, be continued as long as it is possible to do so musically.

Example:

Subject and Countersubject

Stretto.

272. In the above example it can be seen that:

1. The entries are equidistant, with subject and answer appearing every two bars;

2. Subject and answer were interrupted only when it was impossible to continue them;

3. The fourth entry presents the answer in its entirety. This is what should generally be done when, in a stretto with four entries, the subject and answer have been interrupted in the first three.

However, as will be seen later, this rule is usually applied only in the first and last or next-to-last stretto in the fugue.

Note once more that each time the theme has had to be interrupted, it has been replaced either by the countersubject (modified if necessary) or by figures taken from the countersubject.

Interruption of Subject and Answer.

273. Case III. The subject is such that it can in no way be continued after the entry of the answer.

In this case, it is absolutely necessary to interrupt it for the entry of the answer. The part is continued, if possible, by using the discarded fragment of the subject at another pitch or by using the countersubject or figures taken from the countersubject. But in no case may one introduce figures which have not been used in the exposition of the fugue. If it is impossible to do otherwise, however, one may use melodic or rhythmic ideas derived from these figures, even though not reproducing them exactly.

Example:

Subject — (C. FRANCK)

a)

b) **Reversed stretto with closer entries than the preceding one.**

One can see from the third bar of example (a), in the tenor part, that, in this type of stretto, one may modify the subject or answer when necessary to obtain a better musical effect. The A-flat used here in the answer (third bar, third beat) should be A-natural. It is preferable to alter it to avoid the feeling of false relation with the preceding bar.

Close Stretto to be kept in One Key.

274. In this respect we cannot advise our students too strongly that, when they have to deal with a four-part stretto with rather close entries, they must avoid modulating with each entry. They will have to learn to arrange their parts melodically and harmonically in such a way that, from the ensemble of the four entries, there arises a feeling of one tonality and not of a passage alternating from the tonic key to the dominant key and vice versa.

One must not forget that it is to a great extent from such small "tricks of the trade" as this that one learns craftsmanship.

Harmonic Agreement of the Entries

275. An observation of great importance is still to be made with regard to the preceding examples and cases:

One must take care not to introduce the answer against the subject and vice versa unless the first note of the new entry is in harmonic agreement with what precedes.

It is therefore imperative not to abandon the subject at a point where it implies harmonies too distant from those of the head of the answer. On the contrary, one should choose, if possible, a note common to both; or, if the two notes are different, one that belongs to the same chord.

Free Strettos

276. Case IV. Strettos are formed by combinations of subject and answer (canonic or not) at intervals other than the normal, or of subject and subject, or again of answer and answer.

These strettos are called free strettos.

Farther on (Sections 283 ff.) will be found all the examples relative to this type of stretto, which is analyzed in detail in those sections.

277. We are going to give examples of the process of analyzing a subject in order to establish the various strettos.

In the exposition, it is known that the answer is introduced only after the subject has completed its entry in one of the voices.

Example:

278. However, if this subject is tried against the answer, it can be seen that one can, without interrupting the former, introduce the latter at different distances coming closer and closer to the head of the subject. To do this one proceeds by trial and error, trying to introduce the answer on one beat or another of the last bar of the subject. Then, beat by beat, measure by measure, one proceeds in the same way coming back to the head of the subject. Example:

Each one of these combinations constitutes a complete two-part canonic stretto between subject and answer.

279. In addition to cases similar to the preceding ones in which subject and answer can be used in their entirety in canon, there are others in which the canon is incomplete, that is, in which the subject must be interrupted at a given moment while the answer continues (Sec. 271).

Example:

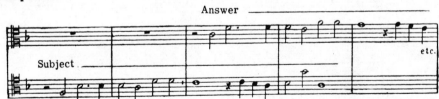

Here one can see that it is impossible to continue the subject at the same time as the answer.

280. Certain subjects either do not give canonic strettos or give them only with the help of a supplementary harmonic part. It goes without saying that, in a fugue, this filling-in part should always be written in contrapuntal style and, in a stretto, taken, as far as possible, from the head of the subject.

Supplementary Harmonic Part.

281. Other subjects (Sec. 270) give canonic strettos beginning only with the answer. Finally, some give not only canonic strettos in normal order, that is, beginning with the subject, but also reversed canonic strettos, that is, beginning with the answer.

Here are two reversed canonic strettos which the preceding subject gives. Note that the first needs at least three parts; and the second, four, with the answer in the bass and the subject in the soprano.

It should be understood that the parts added here have been added only to indicate the possible harmonization of the passage and do not presume to be a finished version.

282. The following subject gives the two forms of canonic stretto in the correct way for two parts:

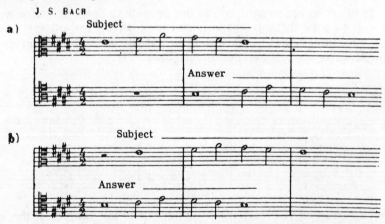

One can see that it is useful to find canonic strettos beginning with the answer and to ascertain, when they seem deficient at first glance, whether these deficiencies cannot be corrected by adding a part to fill out the harmony.

283. In addition to canonic strettos, a subject may be capable of giving canons at different intervals with itself (Sec. 276). Every subject should be analyzed from this point of view — as well as the answer — by trying canons at all intervals and at every distance from the head of the subject or of the answer. Often, in fact, the answer, by virtue of the changes brought about by mutation or modulation, differs enough from the subject to lend itself to its own particular canonic combinations.

284. Continuing the analysis of the preceding subject, we find the following canons:

a) Canon of the subject at the fifth below

b) Canon of the subject at the octave above

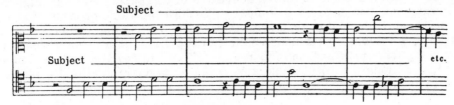

c) Canon of the subject at the seventh below

d) Canon of the answer at the sixth below

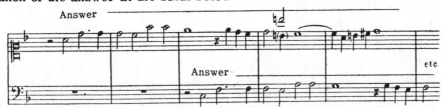

e) Canon of the subject and the answer at the sixth above

285. At this point, several important observations can be made concerning the preceding strettos.

1. The answer may enter at any distance whatsoever from the head of the subject; one need not be concerned as to whether the strong and weak beats of one coincide with those of the other — as is the case in the exposition.

2. The use of canons at various intervals implies necessarily that, in the stretto, one can modulate to neighboring keys and make transitory modulations to distant keys.

3. Note in the examples of Sec. 284 that it may be necessary (as happens often) to change the accidentals [last measure of the subject in (b) and (c)].

4. The stretto (e) in the preceding section opposes weak and strong beats, or, as the old treatises say, "per arsin et thesin" (or "in thesi et arsi"). The former theorists attached great importance to this kind of stretto, the closest kind of all, and considered it absolutely indispensable in the fugue. With modern subjects it is rare that one can use it. But it is good to point it out, so that, if the case should arise, the student may take the opportunity to turn it to account.

286. All the strettos shown above are in two parts. For the fugue with a greater number of parts, one must go through the same process of analysis with three or four parts, or more. Actually, it is rare that subjects which are given at the École lend themselves to canonic strettos in three or four parts; these combinations are, in fact, rather difficult to realise, and the melodic design of modern subjects, too often deficient in character, is ill adapted to multiple canons if one wishes to preserve their configuration.

Entries to be at Equal Distances.

287. A preliminary observation is to be made on the subject of strettos in more than two parts:

The voices should enter at distances equal to the one which separates the first entry of the answer from the head of the subject (Sec. 272).

This rule should be observed strictly for the first and last strettos. For the others, it is not as strict, and it often occurs in a stretto that entries are made at varying distances.

288. When — and this is the most frequent case — the subject and answer cannot be used in canon in four voices, one must abandon the subject at the moment when the answer enters, or several notes later, and vice versa.

In this case, we recall (Sections 271-273) that, if one absolutely cannot continue to use a fragment of the subject, however small it may be, at the same time as the head of the answer, one should try as much as possible to have the counterpoint bring in this fragment at another pitch level, so as not to create the impression that the theme has stopped in one of the parts.

If that cannot be done, then one should take the countersubject and try to superimpose it upon the answer. This is the section of the fugue that requires the most work and the most ingenuity.

289. To set up strettos in four parts for the subject studied in the preceding sections, we shall take up, one by one, the various two-part combinations.

Here are the dispositions which we can get with them. Let us note first that these plans are not final, and represent only preparatory work, without prejudice in any way to the final form of the stretto. In fact, all the following combinations are given in the main key of the subject. They should serve only as a preliminary guide to the preparation of the ensemble, and, considering their great number, it is not likely that all can be used. It is nevertheless highly important that this preparation be done as completely as possible.

Dispositions in four parts of examples given in Sections 278 ff.

Preliminary Dispositions for a Stretto in Four Parts

b) (§ 278$\underline{^b}$)

c) (§ 278$\underline{^c}$)

d) (§ 278ᵈ)

e) (§ 279)

f) (§ 281ᵃ)

g) (§ 281b)

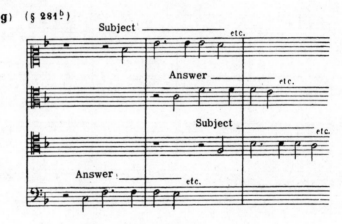

Interruption of Subject and Answer.

290. All the strettos cited in the preceding section fall into the category of canonic strettos or true strettos, even though their entries are not always complete — since subject or answer have to be interrupted in a majority of cases. From these examples one may conclude that:

In a stretto, the successive entries need have only the first bars or even the first notes of subject and answer, with the exception, however, of the last entry which must be complete (Sections 264-272).

291. In practice, as we shall see later, the above rule is applied only to the first and last stretto. The others are generally treated more freely. This is done so as not to lengthen the fugue needlessly unless the subject is very short or gives varied canonic strettos in several parts.

Stretto with Asymmetrical Entries.

292. We shall also see subsequently how all the preliminary plans may be utilized, when they are numerous, by combining them with one another, and by having strettos with non-equidistant entries (Sec. 287).

The reversed stretto that follows is an example of this. It is the realization in four parts of the example cited (Sec. 282b).

293. Here, even if there is asymmetry in the stretto as a whole, one may note that pairs of entries occur at equal distances. An arrangement of this kind is always desirable when a stretto with non-equidistant entries is composed.

Moreover, we shall see later that there is a special type of fugue based on this arrangement. Numerous examples of it are found in Bach, Handel, Mozart, and Mendelssohn.

294. It would be superfluous at this point to go through the above process with four-part dispositions of all the examples given in Sec. 284. It is enough to take the last one (284e, _per arsin et thesin_), to show to what extent one may tighten up entries to bring the fugue to a conclusion.

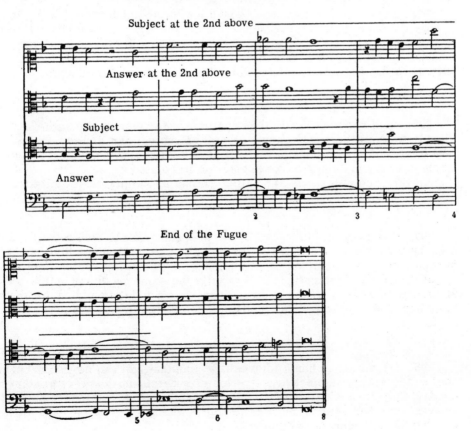

295. In the above example, the bass could have had a complete entry. We modified it purposely, beginning with the third bar, in order to obtain a better realization and a more logical final cadence.

Actually, if we realized the canon strictly in four parts, we would be carried into a tonality that is foreign to the main key of the subject.

Note that, in order to realize the canon strictly, we are twice obliged to flat the E of the answer in the alto part.

With such a realization, one modulates to the subdominant key. In order to end the fugue in a natural manner in the main key, it would be necessary to transpose all of it down a fourth or up a fifth. In this way, the canon could be used in four parts to introduce a pedal on the dominant of the main key, with the pedal immediately preceding the conclusion of the fugue.

Nomenclature of Strettos.

296. In the school fugue, it is customary to restrict the name stretto to closely-knit imitations (canonic or not) of subject and answer in their normal intervallic relationship, that is, at the fifth above or the fourth below, whether in the main key of the subject or in related keys.

All other combinations are called canons or simply close imitations.

Strettos of the Countersubject.

297. A treatment analogous to the preceding one is also carried out for the countersubject. We look for various strettos and canons that can be used in four voices, either alone or combined with strettos of subject and answer.

Since these combinations are exactly the same as those which we have studied with regard to the subject, there is no point in giving examples of them here. For practice, the student should be guided by the preceding analyses.

Strettos with Subject and Countersubject Combined

298. On the other hand, interesting combinations can be made by introducing the countersubject into strettos of subject and answer, whether it is used simply in a single voice during the successive entries of subject and answer, or — and this is most desirable — whether it can be used in double canon with the canon of the subject.

However, it should be noted that the latter will be possible only with very short subjects and countersubjects. With a subject of any length, it is virtually impossible for the countersubject to be introduced into such combinations other than by fragments.

Example:

a) **Well-Tempered Clavier, II, Fugue 9**

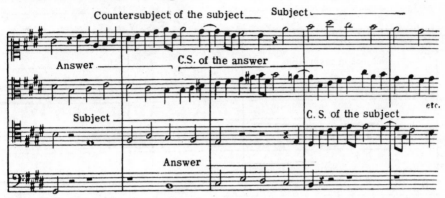

b) **Well-Tempered Clavier, I, Fugue 4**

299. In example (a), the countersubject of the subject is used in its entirety with the canon of answer and subject and ends during the third entry. In the meantime, the countersubject of the answer has entered, beginning on the third beat of the second bar. If Bach had made the last two entries at the same distance as the first two — that is, at a half-bar — he would have had to interrupt the countersubject of the answer. It is very likely that this is not the reason that led him to make the fourth entry at an irregular distance. He did it rather for purely musical reasons.

Example (b) is a model of close combination between the stretto of the subject and the stretto of the countersubject. It can serve as a prototype from which to build this kind of stretto using the head of the subject and the head of the countersubject. If one will consider the subject and countersubject cited here as the beginnings of a more extended subject and countersubject, one will have a perfect example of what a canonic stretto can be, with a fragment of the countersubject as well as the subject used in canonic imitation.

**Stretto in
Inversion**

300. The subject may be inverted — as well as the answer or the countersubject — and form strettos in inversion.

Example:

a) Well-Tempered Clavier, II, Fugue 22 (stretto in canon at the second and seventh below)[1]

b) Ibid., I, Fugue 8 (canon at the third and the octave)

301. In the preceding example (b), the two voices not involved in the canon are not written in just any fashion whatsoever, but participate intimately in the stretto as a whole. All the figures used have been taken either from the subject or from other fragments of the exposition treated in real or rhythmic imitations.

In the soprano we have, in (I), imitation of the subject with opposed ac-

---

1. See the analysis of the exposition of this subject in Sections 197 ff.

cents; in (II), a fragment of the subject in direct motion; in (III), a fragment
of a free part of the exposition; in (IV), rhythmic imitation of the end of the
subject; in (VIII), imitation of the end of the subject in direct motion.

The tenor begins in (V) with a rhythmic imitation of the third bar of the
subject; in the second bar (VI) it uses the rhythm which the soprano picks up
in (IV) in inversion; in (VII) there is a rhythmic imitation of the second figure of the subject in direct motion, etc.

302. A stretto can also consist of inversion in some parts and direct
motion in others:

a) Well-Tempered Clavier, II, Fugue 22 (canon at the second and sixth below
in inversion)

*Stretto in
Direct Motion
and Inversion*

b) J. S. Bach, Fugue for Organ in C major

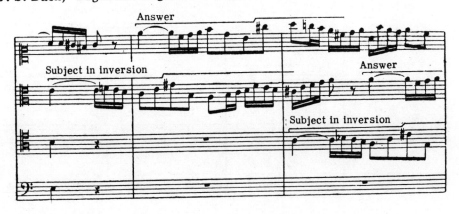

303. The comments which were made in Sec. 301 apply equally to the structure of the preceding examples. The student will take note of this in analyzing example (a) and referring, in regard to his analysis, to Sections 196 ff.

As to example (b), note that the first four entries are in alternately equidistant pairs. The first part of the stretto has the subject in inversion combined with the answer in direct motion. The last two entries are in inverted order. Here the subject is in direct motion and the answer, in inversion. All the subsidiary figures are taken from the subject or the answer, in direct motion or in inversion. One of them

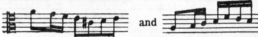

keeps coming back and, used successively in all the voices, is nothing but a modification of the answer in direct motion and in inversion.

Stretto in Diminution.

304. The use of diminution is very common in strettos. Besides the fact that most subjects easily lend themselves to it, diminution has the added advantage of allowing entries to be introduced very close together even when the subject is used in its entirety.

This device is used both in direct motion and in inversion.

305. The following example, taken from the Bach fugue already cited, (Well-Tempered Clavier, II, Fugue 9),

furnishes an excellent model of a stretto in which all the parts are in diminution.

306. More variety, however, may be given to a stretto by having the diminution against the original time-values of the subject, and by making simultaneous use of inversion and direct motion to increase the contrast.

Contrapunctus VI, of J. S. Bach's Art of Fugue, has a series of strettos based upon this type of combination. We give an outline of them here. Students will derive much benefit from what follows it they will put this fugue into open score and analyze it as much from the special point of view of this section as from the viewpoint of composition and voice-leading in general.

It is quite true that few subjects given for school fugues lend themselves to many combinations of this type. Quite often, however, with this method of analysis, one manages to find some in subjects which, at first glance, would not seem to offer any.

The original subject of this fugue of Bach's is the following:

c)

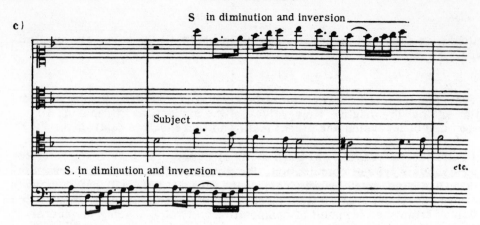

d)

e)

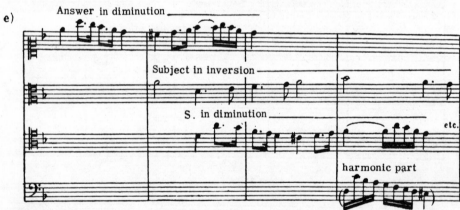

f)

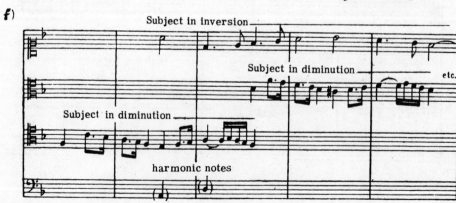

g)

307. In these examples we have tried to isolate the essential parts of the stretto, eliminating the subsidiary parts, so as to make the procedure easier to grasp and to provide the student with the means for analyzing similar combinations. We have limited ourselves to pointing out the harmonic basses of Bach's realization whenever it seemed necessary.

308. There is no point in analyzing these various examples in detail here. The student should have sufficient practice by now to do this for himself. We shall only give some indications of the most interesting points in these remarkable combinations.

Examples (a), (b), and (c) make use of the subject in its original form: in (a), the subject, in diminution, forms a canon in inversion and direct motion with the original subject.

Example (b) begins with the answer in diminution and inversion. In (c), there is a canon between the original subject and the subject in diminution and inversion.

Examples (d) and (e), respectively, are inversions of examples (a) and (b), in this respect: that what is in direct motion in the first is in inversion in the second, and vice versa.

The same relationships exist between examples (c) and (f) except that the canons do not begin at the same distance from the head of the subject and are not at the same interval.

Finally, example (g) reproduces at different intervals the same disposition as (f): in (g), the tenor picks up the head of the subject again in diminution in the bar before the last.

309. Augmentation, the opposite of diminution, has as its effect the wider separation of the entries. Consequently, augmentation is used in the fugue,

Stretto in Augmentation

and principally in the stretto, only as an element of contrast, to make the close entries of the subject in the other voices stand out more, whether it appears there in its original state or in diminution, by direct motion or in inversion, or with a combination of the two.

310. The very nature of augmentation permits it to be used only in a single voice, or at the very most, in two, and in the latter case only when the subject in augmentation lends itself to double canon with the original subject. Such a situation arises very seldom. Furthermore, the combination must not harm the musical effect of the fugue, and must not slow down the movement or the interest, a major defect at the moment of conclusion.

311. In certain strettos, one may use the subject, in augmentation, only in imitations entering close to the head of the subject or answer in their original form.

The subject analyzed above (Sections 278a, b) might give us, as an example of this type, the following combinations:

312. Along this line of thought, it is conceivable that there is an infinite number of dispositions, varying according to the subjects and the devices employed, such as diminution, direct motion, inversion, retrograde, etc.

Canonic Stretto in Direct Motion and Inversion and with Augmentation

313. When the subject lends itself, one may use it, or the answer, in direct motion or in inversion with its original time-values, while another voice has it in augmentation.

The works of Bach, Mozart, and Handel offer numerous examples of this type of combination. We shall give two examples from Bach:

---

1. The notes in parentheses are the notes of the simple harmonic bass.

a) **Well-Tempered Clavier, II, Fugue 2**

b) **Fugue for Organ in C major**

314. Contrapunctus VII of Bach's Art of Fugue is based entirely on the use of augmentation combined with the subject either in its original time-values or in diminution, in direct motion or in inversion. This fugue could be cited in its entirety, but we shall give only two excerpts, at the same time advising students to study and analyze the entire fugue carefully.

Stretto in Augmentation and Diminution Combined.

It is based on the following subject.

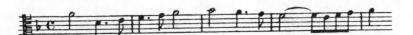

Subject in diminution and

Subject' in diminution and inversion

etc.

inversion

In example (a), the subject in augmentation is accompanied in two parts by a canon at the octave of the subject, inverted, in its original time-values, with the fourth part based entirely on the final figure of the subject in diminution.

In example (b), the other parts have strettos and fragments of the subject in diminution, while the subject enters in augmentation and inversion.

315. Of all the devices used in the stretto, retrograde (with or without inversion) is the least used. Very few subjects can be turned backwards without being rendered completely unrecognizable.

Stretto in Retrograde.

The way to treat this device in combination is exactly the same as for the preceding combinations.

The examples cited in Sec. 249 can be considered as strettos in which the subject is used simultaneously in its original state, in simple retrograde, and in retrograde inversion. We refer the student to it.

316. Here, then, have been presented the various kinds of combinations

which can enter into the composition of a stretto. Though in most cases all of them do not find employment, they must be looked into with the greatest care before one writes a fugue.

317. Before demonstrating how one carries out these various procedures in constructing a stretto, we must consider a device which, at least in the school fugue, is obligatory. We refer to the _pedal_. Its study is the subject of the following chapter.

CHAPTER IX

The Pedal[1]

318. The pedal is that part of the fugue which gets its name from the harmonic device which is the basis of it. It consists in sustaining the same note in one or more parts for a certain number of bars.

Definitions

319. The pedal can therefore be either simple or multiple. It generally comes on the dominant or on the tonic. In some exceptional cases, however, it can be on some other degree of the scale.

Harmonic Rules of the Pedal.

320. The rules that apply to the pedal from the purely harmonic point of view are the same in fugue as in harmony; that is, a pedal may begin and end only as a consonance. In entering, it must be a constituent, consonant note of the harmony, and it may be abandoned only as a consonance or as a consonant bass of a dissonant chord. In certain cases, the pedal on the dominant may stop at the moment in which it forms a dissonance which is prepared and resolved normally. Immediately after it has entered, however, it becomes more or less foreign to all the harmonies brought about by the voice-leading of the other parts and may, consequently, form any kind of unprepared dissonance with them. We point this out only as a reminder, since students who have been working with fugue have been familiar with the harmonic employment of the pedal for a long time.

321. One of the great advantages of the pedal on the tonic or on the dominant is that the various related keys can be used while, at the same time, the main key of the fugue is confirmed. It therefore contributes to tightening up the thread of the musical discourse and bringing renewed interest to it.

Role of the Pedal.

322. This quality of the pedal permits it to be used to prepare the first entries of the stretto if it is placed immediately before the first stretto, as will be seen in the following chapters. Then, however, it is used on the dominant or, more rarely, on some other degree of the scale. The tonic pedal is reserved for the conclusion of the fugue itself.

---

1. See Editor's Introduction

323. Here are the parts to which the pedal is entrusted, in the order of their frequency of employment.

1. The bass (pedal below)
2. The upper part (pedal above)
3. One of the inner parts (pedal in an inner voice)

Double Pedal

324. The pedal may also be doubled in the same part (usually the bass) or used simultaneously in the two outer parts. In such a case, it is usual to find the tonic pedal and the dominant pedal used simultaneously. It is also common, however, to double either one or the other.

Place of the Pedal.

325. Following the point in the fugue at which the pedal enters, the nature and flow of the other parts is different. If the pedal comes before the stretto, it will enter during an episode and this episode will be continued over the pedal. If, on the other hand, it enters toward the end of the stretto section, it can be used with other strettos, canonic or not, but in any case with the entries very close together.

326. As the pedal is the part of the fugue in which the most freedom is left to the student, it is absolutely impossible to formulate exact rules on the subject. The method of treating it depends primarily upon the ingenuity of the composer. All that can be said is that all the kinds of episodes or strettos that we have studied so far can be employed over a pedal.

327. From a purely musical point of view, the important thing is for the pedal to be brought about naturally. One must feel it coming in some way. The musician must provoke in his hearer this special sensation, impossible to define, which is given by the entry of a well-manipulated pedal, either on the dominant to prepare the conclusion of the fugue, or on the tonic, to carry out the conclusion itself.

328. Without stopping at this very important last point, to which we shall return eventually, we shall give several models of different types of pedals.
The following pedal, on the dominant, is an example of an episode over a pedal in which each part imitates itself. It illustrates, moreover, the type of combination most frequently employed with a pedal, for it is the one which allows the closest-knit patterns (diatonic or chromatic) to prepare for the entry of the stretto.

J. S. Bach, Art of Fugue, Contrapunctus VIII
Episode introducing the entry of the pedal

Pedal (on the dominant of the 4th degree of the main key)

329. The following example shows a dominant pedal with a free stretto in
ree parts over it. The pedal ends, as in the preceding example, with a
assage in which each part imitates itself.

Mendelssohn, Organ Fugue, op. 37, no. 3

330. Here is an admirable example of a tonic pedal over which a double stretto in inversion and direct motion is used. It is the end of the great fugue for organ in C major by J. S. Bach which we have already cited several times.

Note that, although this fugue is written mainly for four voices, the pedal is treated in five voices. This addition of a voice is also permitted in the school fugue in order to obtain a greater fullness of sonority at the end of the fugue, or to supply a fifth part if the combinations of strettos require it.

(In certain cases of double pedal, writing in six parts is also found and permitted in a school fugue of four voices. Some examples of this kind will be given later.)

331. The end of the fugue for organ in G major by J. S. Bach, already cited, presents an example of a tonic pedal in the upper voice, to which is added, in the last three bars, another tonic pedal in the bass.

tonic pedal above

tonic pedal below

332. Sometimes the pedal note, instead of being sustained, is repeated in a rhythmic pattern or else is woven into a melodic pattern which brings it back at equal time intervals. This is what is called the ornamented pedal.

Ornamented Pedal

This rhythm or design is always borrowed from a characteristic figure of the subject or countersubject, or from one of their rhythms.

333. In the following examples, you will find various models of this type of pedal, a type which may be varied at the will of the composer.

In (a) the tonic pedal, in an inner voice, is ornamented rhythmically by the leading tone.

In (b) the pedal, in the bass, has a rhythm borrowed from the main theme.

Example (c) shows a pedal on the second degree of the main key. The pedal is at first ornamented by the upper auxiliary tone and then continues with a trill, beginning with the second bar.

The treatment of example (d) is very common in fugues for piano or organ.

In (e), the rhythm of the pedal alternates with that of the main figure.

The pedal in example (f) is more complex. First of all, it is double, one part sustained, the other figured with a rhythm taken from the countersubject. Then it bcomes internal.

Finally, in (g), the pedal imitates the rhythm of a fragment of the subject.

a) J. S. Bach, Fugue for Organ in C major

pedal in an inner voice

Subject

etc

b) J. S. Bach,   Prelude for Organ in F minor

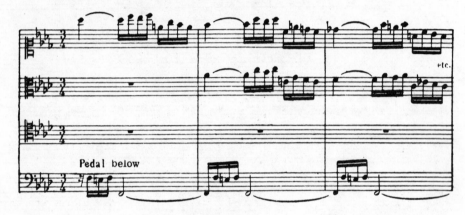

Pedal below

etc.

c) J. S. Bach,   Fugue for Organ in D minor

Canon at the octave below

Pedal below

Canon at the 4th above

Canon at the 15th below

etc.

d) J. S. Bach, Fugue for Organ in B minor

e) Prelude of the same fugue

f) Schumann, Fugue no. 6 on the name of Bach

g) Mendelssohn, Quartet, op. 81

Multiple Ornamented Pedal.

334. In J. S. Bach's Passacaglia for Organ there is a curious employment of an ornamented pedal that is simple, double, and quadruple, forming
rhythmic imitations. Although, strictly speaking, this passage is not fugue
composition, and although it is closer to just contrapuntal style, we feel we
have the right to cite it, if only to awaken the attention of the student to the
possibilities of some interesting dispositions that can be found with the aid
of the ornamented pedal.

335. An interesting combination, in which the pedal is used successively in the three upper parts—and one which could be applied to the school fugue—is to be found in the Ninth Quartet of Beethoven.[1]

1. This example is cited here only as a possibility and not as a pedal typical of the school fugue.

336. Students should analyze the preceding examples carefully from the
point of view of melodic and harmonic structure and of the disposition of the
imitations, and in this analysis they should proceed as we did in the analyses
of episodes and strettos. In addition, in the fugues cited farther on, they will
find excellent examples of what a pedal in the school fugue should be. From
studying these models, they will learn to compose pedals on themes which
they can create themselves, or else they may borrow either from examples
cited in the preceding chapters or from among the fugue subjects given at
the end of this volume.

337. We have finished analyzing the various elements that comprise the
fugue. We are now going to put them to work and make some kind of synthe-
sis out of them, studying the overall construction of the fugue.

CHAPTER X

Modulations of the Fugue

338. With the exposition (or counter exposition, if there is one) ends the first part of the fugue. Following immediately, there begin those developments which constitute its second part. These developments, as we have seen, are formed by the episodes that periodically bring back the subject, answer, and countersubject.

339. In order to avoid that monotony which would result from the constant reiteration of the original tonality, the subject is in a different key at each reappearance. But, just as one gives the fugue melodic and rhythmic unity by limiting oneself to the material used in the exposition, so tonal unity is given to it by modulating only to keys related to the main key, that is, to keys whose signatures differ from that of the main key by only one sharp or flat more or less.

340. For any given key the related keys are:

a) In the major mode:
>   the minor key on the second degree (supertonic)
>   the minor key on the third degree (mediant)
>   the major key on the fourth degree (subdominant)
>   the major key on the fifth degree (dominant)
>   the minor key on the sixth degree (submediant or relative
>   minor)

b) In the minor mode
>   the major key on the third degree (mediant or relative major)
>   the minor key on the fourth degree (subdominant)
>   the minor key on the fifth degree (dominant)
>   the major key on the sixth degree (submediant)
>   the major key on the seventh degree unaltered (subtonic)

341. In a fugue, the exposition, counter exposition, and the first and last

Related Keys.

strettos must always be in the main key of the subject.

Order of Modulations.

343. In a free fugue, the number and order of modulations depend only upon the fancy of the composer. The same applies to the number and length of the episodes.

In examinations or musical competitions, it is customary to observe the following order of modulations:

Subjects in the Major Mode.

344. If the subject is in the major mode, the first modulation is to the sixth degree of the main key, where there is an entry of the subject. The answer to this entry naturally leads the fugue to the new key of the third degree.

With the assistance of an episode, one modulates next to the key of the fourth degree, in which only the subject is used, because the answer would bring the fugue back to the main key. By means of a short episode, or, if possible, without any transition at all, one modulates to the key of the second degree, in which there is only one entry, either of the subject or of the answer. A new episode is constructed, more extended that the preceding ones, in the course of which the subject enters in the dominant key. This episode leads to the first stretto.

The episode may terminate on a pedal that is rather extended; either on the dominant (as is most generally the case) or on some other degree. And it may lead directly to the stretto or be separated from it by a short pause. This pause is generally on the dominant. It may, however, be on some other degree so long as the stretto can be linked to it in a natural way.

Subjects in the Minor Mode.

345. If the subject is in the minor mode, the number of episodes and the method of arriving at the stretto are the same as in the major mode. The order of modulations, however, is slightly different. After the exposition, an episode leads to an entry of the subject in the key of the third degree (relative major key) and its answer then modulates to the key of the unaltered seventh degree. From this point, there is a modulation to the key of the fourth degree, to which the sixth degree serves as answer. Finally, one last episode, during which the subject may enter in the dominant key, leads to the first stretto.

Length of the Episodes.

346. No hard and fast rule can be given for the lengths of the episodes which modulate to related keys. An average, however, can be set up in accordance with the length of the subject and the exposition.

If one assumes an average length of from four to six bars for subjects in competitions, the exposition, depending upon whether the entries of subject and answer succeed each other without interruption or are separated by one or more codettas, should be from 16 to 24 bars.

347. In proportion, one would be inclined to give the various episodes the following dimensions. The table is set up for the major mode, but it can be applied, except for the order of modulations, to fugues in the minor mode:

Designation of the Parts of the Fugue	Number of Bars varying approximately	
	from	to
Exposition	16	24
Episode I	8	12
Subject at the 6th degree	4	6
Answer (3rd degree)	4	6
Episode II	10	16
Subject at the 4th degree	4	6
Transition	2	4
Subject or Answer at the 2nd degree	4	6
Episode III	14	20
From beginning of fugue to stretto . . .	66	100

348. The above dimensions should be considered as the extremes between which the lengths of the various parts of the fugue should fall. If the stretto is kept to the same proportions, there will be from 100 to 150 bars in the entire fugue. These figures, though they are not absolute, appear to us to include any fugue which is not too short nor too extended.

349. Whatever the case, these proportions are purely arbitrary. So are the order, the number, and the choice of modulations set up for the school fugue. Nothing in the fugues composed by the Bachs and Handels, the Mozarts and Mendelssohns, authorizes anyone to consider these prescriptions as exact, or, for that matter, to grant them any value whatever. For in the works of the masters no example can be found that can be considered as even the simplest confirmation of these rules. Tradition alone has set them up and made them observed and respected. In our turn, therefore, let us respect them in the name of tradition, but let us be careful to give them only the importance assigned to them in competitions or examinations.

350. In disregard of the rule, one may have the subject modulate briefly from the main major mode to the parallel minor mode and vice versa: if the main mode of the subject is minor, transform it for a moment into the major mode. If, for example, a subject is in A minor, the key of A major could be used briefly, and vice versa.

This license, which the masters have illustrated in admirable fashion, is allowed in school only to bring the subject back to the main key, or else, in the minor mode, for the conclusion of the fugue. But it must not be abused because, in this case, there are always three accidentals of difference from the signature of the main key. Let only one be authorized!

351. For the same reason, the answer is never used when a subject in the major mode modulates to the keys of the third or fifth degrees, or when a subject in the minor mode modulates to the keys of the fifth or seventh degrees (the latter unaltered). The reason is easier to understand in this than in the preceding case because these answers would make the fugue modulate to keys from which it would be difficult to return to the main key in a natural manner.

352. Certain subjects do not lend themselves to transposition to the key parallel to the main key. A subject in the major mode may not be very musical or else may be unrecognizable in the minor mode, and vice versa.

Subject in the Parallel Key

353. Such difficulties generally arise from intervals which are made difficult of intonation by the transposition from one mode to another. Then again, in some subjects there occur, as a result of this transposition, unharmonic intervals or intervals of doubtful tonality. Or even still, one may encounter very real difficulties when harmonizing a subject transposed in this way. Formerly, in such cases, students were forbidden to use the subject in the parallel mode without modifying it or truncating it. Today, one prefers to avoid the problem, and in an examination or competition, the student might find himself in a difficult position if he used this former indulgence.

354. The best method of procedure in all cases is as follows: It consists in considering any alteration placed before a note in the subject or implied in the harmony, not as chromatic, but as tonal, that is, as resulting from a momentary modulation of a fragment of the subject to a new tonality.

In transposing the subject to the mode opposite that of the main mode, one will get the most faithful version of the transposed subject if one is careful that the relation of temporary modulations to the new mode is the same as it was in the original mode.

Example:

In this example, note that the subject, in the main mode, modulates briefly to the key of the mediant. In transposing it to the relative major key (C major) the corresponding fragment has modulated to the key of the mediant of C major (E minor) to end the subject in the key of the dominant of C major.[1]

_____

1. Subjects of this type should be strictly forbidden. There is no example in which the

355. Here is another example of the same type:

Subject in the major mode (E♭)   implied modulation to the subdominant
of E♭ major

Subject transposed to the relative minor   implied modulation to the subdominant
mode (C minor)   of C min.

The following example, purely theoretical, is more complex:

Subject in the major mode (C major)

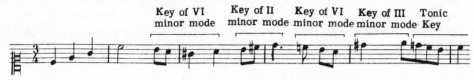

Its transposition to the relative minor mode will give this:

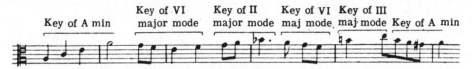

and not this, which, at first glance, might appear accurate because the intervals coincide exactly, semitone by semitone.

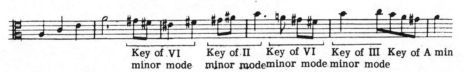

If one is guided by the harmonic relationship of the various degrees of
the subject to the main key, one will realize that the real solution is the first,
and that in the former alone do the harmonic relationships of the implied
tonalities correspond exactly in both modes to the basic tonality of the subject.

There is no need to add that this series of modulations is only theoretical and that in reality a subject would not pass through these different tonalities.

356. In any case, when composing a fugue, one should be forewarned
about these difficulties and pitfalls, and one should choose subjects that

---

theme of a sonata or symphony, or even a simple melody belongs simultaneously to the two
modes, major and minor. It is even more important for a fugue subject not to oscillate constantly back and forth between the modes. It is obvious that, no matter how well written a
fugue may be on such a subject, it can never be any good musically. When we hear it, we will
never know which mode, or even what key we are in at a given moment. Such subjects can
only distort the student's judgment if he is not shown what is defective about them from the
point of view of musical logic.

sound correct, integral, and identically similar in both modes.

357. The student will find, in the chapter which gives the general summary, all the examples relative to the application of modulations. .

CHAPTER XI

Construction of the Stretto Section

358. In every type of fugue, only two parts of the stretto section should have the same disposition, the first and last strettos.

359. Both should be in the main key of the fugue, and consist of four entries, with only the last entry absolutely required to present the main theme (subject or answer) in its entirety.

The first and last strettos differ from each other only in the disposition of the entries, which are at closer distances in the second than in the first.

360. All the other parts of the stretto vary according to the subjects. One may modulate in them, and the number of entries is not set in any absolute manner.

361. Theoretically, a stretto, in its overall construction, should be composed entirely of an uninterrupted succession of canons of subject and answer—canons whose entries become closer and closer as one nears the conclusion of the fugue.

In practice, however, it is rarely this way. Very few subjects can be adapted to enough canonic combinations. This lack of combinations is made up for by various devices.

362. One may sum up as follows the various ways of constructing a stretto:

1. The canonic entries of subject and answer follow each other without interruption.

2. Strettos of subject and answer are linked by strettos of the countersubject.

3. Strettos of countersubject and answer are connected by episodes.

Each of these ways of constructing a stretto will be studied separately.

363. Case I. Canons of subject and answer follow each other without interruption:

a. First, one composes a stretto consisting of four entries, as has been explained above (Sections 169-170).

b. Immediately after the first stretto, the second is begun, and it is followed, without interruption, by a third, and so on until the conclusion of the fugue. To avoid monotony, the successive strettos can modulate to several related keys, without, however, losing sight of the main tonality of the fugue.

Example:

Bach, Well-Tempered Clavier, I, Fugue 1

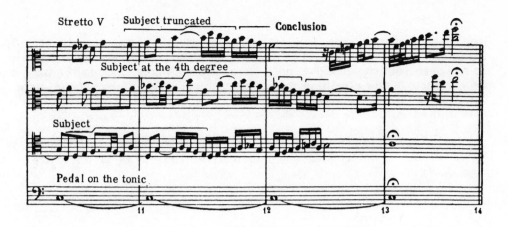

364. At this point, we shall recall an observation already made: The examples that we have quoted from the works of the great masters never follow the established pattern of the school fugue. Consequently, they must not be studied from this point of view, but rather as models of artistic, musical forms. Even in the school fugue one can strive to attain the style and speak the language of the Bachs and Mozarts.

But what must be avoided, above all, are the flat, banal, pat established formulas which have nothing to do with Art. Even when employing the stilted, conventional framework of the school fugue, one can compose music. And, after all, that is what a composer's purpose must always be.

365. Note in the preceding example that, contrary to the rules of the school fugue:

1. The first stretto has a single entry of the subject followed by three entries of the answer;

2. The four entries are made at uneven distances from the head of the subject;

3. The final stretto has only three entries instead of the four it should have according to the rules;

4. The various strettos are presented in an arbitrary order with respect to the degree of closeness of the entries.

366. To sum up, in this example, the analogies we have with what is called the school fugue are very few. They are limited to the employment of a short pedal on the dominant (bars 7, 8) separated by two entries from the tonic pedal over which the conclusion is built.

Such as it is, however, this example should be studied a long time. For it is a perfect model of the real style of the stretto. Students should be inspired by it in their school work, avoiding the few liberties in composition and form which Bach could allow himself but which would be considered reprehensible at the École.

367. Case II. The strettos of subject and answer are separated by strettos of the countersubject.

Alternate Strettos of Subject and Countersubject.

After the first stretto of subject and answer with four required entries has been composed, there follows a first stretto of the countersubject leading to the second stretto of the subject in a related key. This second stretto, as has been pointed out above, need have only two parts, and may or may not be canonic. A new stretto of the countersubject follows this second stretto, followed in turn by a third stretto of the subject, and so on up to the conclusion of the fugue.

368. From this point of view, fugue 5 of the Well-Tempered Clavier, II, by J. S. Bach, is interesting and informative. Here it is in its entirety in open score.

369. First of all, note that, in this fugue, the countersubject (which is not written in double counterpoint) is based on a fragment of the subject:

Since Bach has given it the character and role of a true countersubject, we have no reason for not considering it as such. It is up to the student to apply to the school fugue the principles and the methods of procedure which Bach employs in free style, keeping in mind at the same time, however, academic rules and principles.

The indications given in this fugue are enough to enable the student to analyze it himself. We shall not do this work here.[1]

370. To serve as a comparison, here is another stretto, written by one of my pupils, on a subject whose possibilities of combination have been studied at great length in Sections 277 ff:

Subject by A. Gedalge

1st Stretto

---

1. In this example, note that all the strettos of the countersubject can be characterized as "episodes". This procedure is common in the school fugue and is correct, though, as may be seen in Sections 372 ff., true episodes in the stretto are of an entirely different nature.

1st Stretto of the C.S.(Canonic)

2nd Stretto (Canon of the subject at the 3rd degree)

2nd Stretto of the C.S. (Canonic)

3rd Stretto of the subject at the 2nd degree (Canonic)

4th Stretto of the S. (combined with the C.S. and the subj. in augmentation)
S. augmented

Dominant pedal

5th Stretto (canonic) in 4 voices over a tonic pedal

371. By referring to Sections 277 ff., one can see that this stretto is far from having used most of the combinations which the subject of the fugue lends itself to. He could have composed a more closely knit work by using only strettos of the subject and answer without utilizing canons of the countersubject. For example, the first stretto, instead of being constructed with interrupted entries, would have gained by being presented in the form given in Section 289 (b). The final stretto would also have been more interesting and would have had a more sustained style if it had been composed as indicated in Sections 294-295.

In spite of these few insignificant imperfections, inevitable in a student's work, one will profit from analyzing this stretto and by practicing the composition of similar ones. For this work, students can be guided by the analyses made in Chapter VIII, and, using this same subject, treat it in different combinations.

Episodes in the Stretto.

372. Case III. Strettos of subject and answer are connected by episodes.

Often—and this is the most common case in the school fugue—the subject of a fugue is not adaptable to enough canonic combinations to have strettos of subject and countersubject follow each other uninterruptedly. Then it is customary to introduce episodes between the strettos, whether canonic or with interrupted entries of subject and answer.

373. These episodes are constructed in the same ways as those which precede the stretto, with this slight difference, that their motives should be very short and should come from the head of the subject, the answer, or the countersubject. Furthermore, keeping in mind as much as possible the composition of the stretto, they should be most often canonic, or should at least present a continuous overlapping of entries.

374. In these episodes, one is free to employ all the devices of direct motion, inversion, and retrograde, of augmentation or diminution. But one should bear in mind that the shorter they are, the better they will be. If they are extended too much, they will detract from the interest of the stretto and harm its movement by spacing the entries of subject and answer too far apart.

375. On the other hand, if one is willing to consider the resources of inversion, augmentation, and diminution, which, applied to the subject, constitute true stretto combinations, one will easily realize that there is no need to have recourse to episodes. The 30 or 40 bars that constitute an entire stretto section can be easily filled with a series of strettos constructed in accordance with the aforementioned devices.

376. Here, now, is an example of a school fugue stretto which includes two episodes. It is based on the following subject and countersubject:

STRETTO

14

EPISODE I
Head of the subject (in inversion)

2ⁿᵈ **Stretto** (at the 6th degree) in diminution

EPISODE II   id.   3rd **Stretto**

(canonic)   Answer

377. The analysis shows that the episodes in the preceding stretto are constructed in the same way as those in the second section of the fugue. They differ from them only in the greater brevity of their motives, and by a more tightly-knit construction.

Linking of the Episode with the Strettos.

The melodic plan of the first episode (beginning with the 12th bar) can be described in this way:

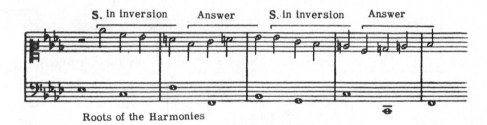

The four voices imitate each other and the free parts are based on the countersubject.

378. In the second episode the main melodic line is in the soprano. The alto and tenor imitate each other. The bass imitates itself.

Note that in this episode:

1. Alto and tenor use imitations of the head of the answer in diminution—imitations identical to those which formed the basis of the preceding stretto.

2. The melodic line of the episode continues uninterrupted in the third stretto so as to lead in a natural manner to the fourth entry of this stretto. Similarly, the free parts continue with imitations of the head of the subject and the head of the answer in diminution, and by direct motion or in inversion.

379. It is a good idea to work out the figures of a stretto episode in such a way that this episode can be continued uninterruptedly by a stretto (canonic or not, free or true). This method of procedure gives much more cohesion to this part of the fugue. The effect is even better if a short episode with the head of the subject in inversion is linked in a natural way to a stretto in direct motion.

The following stretto, on this subject:

is an example of an episode conceived in this manner. Taking the form of a stretto in inversion, this episode leads in a very natural way to the second stretto of the subject, which appears to continue it in this way:

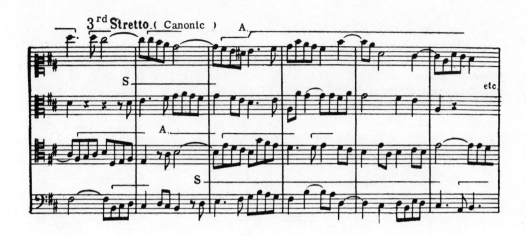

380. In a general way, one may sum up the method of constructing a stretto section for a school fugue as follows:

Overall Construction of the Stretto.

1. **First Stretto:** consisting of four entries (canonic or not), the fourth entry alone presenting the subject in its entirety; accompanied or not by the countersubject: this first stretto is always in the main key of the fugue.

2. **Episode:** (or stretto of the countersubject with at least two entries) leading to a

3. **Second Stretto** of the subject, which may consist of only two entries, in a related key,

4. **Second Episode,** short and closely-knit, or second stretto of the countersubject with entries at closer distances than the first,

5. **Third Stretto** of the subject, which, if it is the last one, should have four entries very close together and be in the main key of the fugue.

This last stretto may be preceded by a pedal on the dominant, and may be over a tonic pedal; or else it may separate the dominant pedal from the tonic pedal.

In each case, it is a good idea to conclude on the tonic pedal or immediately afterwards.

381. There used to be a rule in the school fugue to have the pedal preceded by a reversed stretto, that is, one beginning with the answer. One may still conform to this principle if it adds musical interest, but it is not obligatory.

Reversed Stretto.

Analysis of a Stretto

382. We will now analyze, in its entirety, a stretto written for a school fugue. First, we shall give the exposition. By itself, the subject offers little of musical interest. For this very reason it will serve to show students what can be done with any subject at all, provided only that that subject lends itself to contrapuntal combinations, without which it is impossible to construct a fugue.

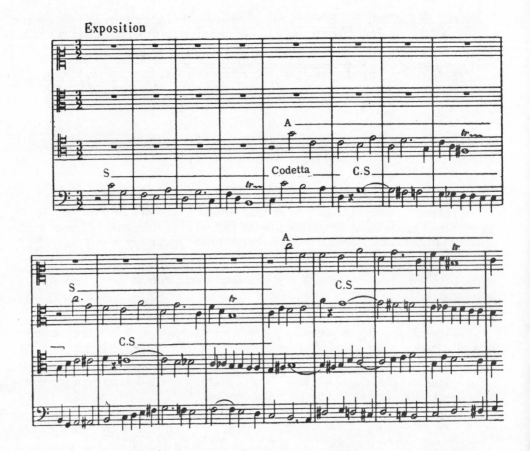

STRETTO

383. If at first we compare the exposition of this fugue with the first stretto, we can see that they differ from each other not only in the disposition of the entries, which are closer together in the latter than in the former, but also in the composition of the parts. In the stretto, the parts make use of fragments of the countersubject in close imitation.

Actually, the first stretto, which is a kind of exposition with the entries more closely-knit, must not resemble the exposition which is at the beginning of the fugue. Such a defect will make it appear as if the fugue itself were beginning over again.

384. In the fourth bar of the stretto, there begins a first episode whose

elements come from the head of the subject and from its codetta. The entries
of the main theme,

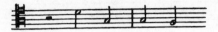

equidistant, come at the distance of one bar, with tenor and alto imitating
each other while the other two parts imitate each other in inversion. The
episode, based on a non-modulating pattern, modulates suddenly to the key
of the dominant in the 17th bar, where the second stretto begins.

385. This stretto, a canon of the answer at the octave, is in two parts.
The other parts use either the answer in diminution (bass, bar 17) or the
head of the subject and the answer, in diminution and inversion (alto and
bass, bars 18 and 19).

The third stretto, closer by one measure than the preceding one, is in the
key of the third degree, and consists of a canon at the octave of the subject
and answer between the alto and tenor.

The fourth stretto is based on a canon of the answer at the fifth above.
This canon is between the bass and tenor and is at the same distance as the
preceding one.

386. The second, third, and fourth strettos follow each other without interruption. An episode of two bars, based on fragments of the subject in diminution, serves as a transition between the fourth and fifth strettos. The
latter begins in three parts; the bass and alto alone continue the canon which
ends on a cadence in the main key leading to a sixth canonic stretto of subject and answer. At the same time there is presented in the two upper parts
an identical stretto, but in diminution.

387. The dominant pedal, on which the sixth stretto ends (bar 42) is of a
more complex nature. It actually uses simultaneously:
1. The subject in diminution
2. The head of the subject in its original time-values
3. Fragments of the countersubject in direct motion or in inversion.
As a matter of fact, it may be considered an episode, extended and tight-
ened up. Its main melodic line up to bar 50 could be reconstructed as follows:

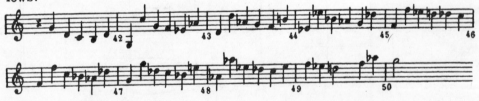

388. Without going into detail concerning the musical composition of this
pedal (since we shall touch on this subject in the following chapter), we shall
note here that this part of the pedal consists of two groups of four bars each
that are harmonically and melodically similar.

389. On the 51st bar there begins, over a double pedal (above and below)
a stretto of the countersubject in canon at the octave, while the bass has the
head of the subject. The pedal moves to the tonic with a deceptive cadence in
bar 57, and over it there is a tight episode based on imitations of the head of
the subject, while the melodic line begun in bar 51 continues in the two soprano parts.

390. The tonic pedal ends at the end of the 62nd bar and after four close entries of subject and answer, in which only the head is used (seventh stretto) one arrives at the conclusion of the fugue with a perfect cadence.

391. By analyzing this stretto even more closely, students will realize that in none of its parts does it have elements foreign to the exposition. From that they will realize that, when one knows how to make use of all the devices of counterpoint, there is no theme which is not suitable for musical development.

392. This stretto, more extended than those usually written in the school fugue, does not use all the available combinations to which the subject lends itself. We therefore urge the student to take this subject and, after having made a methodical analysis of it, analyzing all the canons and imitations of the subject, answer, and countersubject, to compose another stretto that has combinations different from those which have been employed above.

CHAPTER XII

Musical Composition of the Fugue

393. The essential, basic qualities of a well-made fugue are:
1. Continuity of texture
2. Unity of style

394. In order to assure the first of these qualities, continuity of texture, certain theorists have forbidden the perfect cadence in the course of the fugue, reserving it for the conclusion only. Simple common sense suffices to illustrate that this rule is based on erroneous reasoning.

395. Obviously, if one pictures a fugue as a collection of methods destined solely to carry a subject into various keys, one will never get anything but an artificial construction, whose seams will be carefully concealed by the employment of certain harmonic devices well-known to composers. Under these conditions, continuity of texture can be assured only if one abstains completely from perfect cadences. The slightest stop in a work of this nature actually gives the impression of a definite conclusion, a point which one is supposed to reach in the school fugue only after a certain number of convolutions, carefully prearranged and decreed.

396. One's impression will be completely different if the fugue is considered as the development of a musical idea—and by musical idea, one must understand a collection of rhythmic and melodic designs—just as developing a theme musically means to create with the rhythms of which this theme is composed a whole series of new melodic forms derived naturally and logically from each other.

397. Considered from this point of view, the fugue will necessarily emerge for what it really is, once its exposition is terminated: the development of a musical idea by the uninterrupted creation of new melodic forms

derived from this idea and expressed in a style of regular periodic imitation.

In other words, the fugue is nothing more than one long, single episode, with multiple melodic forms, and with imitations that are more and more tightly drawn, periodically bringing back the generating theme in the main key or in other keys.

398. Without exception, it is in this form that all the fugues of the great masters are presented to us; and it is in this respect, above all, that these fugues differ from those given as models in the schools, where one finds an artificial, lifeless collection of bits and pieces, without style—for the employment of formulas does not constitute a style—without melodic line, stripped of any kind of artistic feeling and color. With the masters, however, there is continuity of movement toward a sensible and well-considered end—expression and life, indispensible to every work of art, unity of style with a variety of melodic forms.

The masters have proved that the fugue could be used to **express ideas.** One must not see in it solely a method by which to sift and re-sift **formulas.**

399. Continuity of texture, in the **fugue, can** be assured by observation of this one principle: never allow all the **parts** to rest at the same time.

Continuity of Texture and Continuity in the Melodic Line.

Something even more essential is continuity of the melodic line.

This quality will be attained if one is careful to manage the **transitions** and especially to see that the subject, at each appearance, logically continues the episode which precedes it. Likewise, the free parts which accompany it should prepare for the episode which follows it in a natural manner. This idea can be expressed simply by saying that the two episodes should be joined around the subject, the one beginning as soon as the other ends, as we shall see in the following examples:

J. S. Bach,   Organ Fugue in C Minor

b) same fugue

400. In example (a), from the eighth to the eleventh bar, during the entry of the subject, the soprano and tenor continue the dialogue begun in the preceding episode. Note the expressive harmony (first beat of the tenth bar) on which the bass ends.

In the 12th bar, the tenor, and then the alto, announce the figure of the following episode, which thus begins before the subject is ended.

During a dialogue between soprano and alto, which continues the second episode, the subject, with its head melodically modified, is picked up again by the tenor. This same melodic figure serves (in the 25th bar), as a lead-in for the tenor, to pick up the main motive of the third episode, at the end of which the soprano entry uses the same modified version of the head of the subject.

401. The episode with which example (b) begins is continued uninterruptedly up to the end of the third bar, during which the subject has reentered in the bass. The procedure is the same when, in the seventh bar, the tenor has the answer. In the ninth bar, there is an admirable use of a six-four chord (not forgetting that, no matter how delightful this bar may be, it would not be allowed in an examination or competition).

Employment of the Perfect Cadence. 402. It is understood, of course, that all fugues, like the preceding one, may be written without a cadence. In many cases, it is a good idea, at the end of a melodic period, to pause momentarily. It is then that the perfect cadence may be judiciously employed.

Its use is limited by the following conditions:

1. The subject must enter shortly before the end of the cadence or else immediately after it, so that there is no interruption in the continuity of the melodic line.

2. After a cadence, the subject may reenter only on a note that can be a member of the final chord of the cadence (the harmony itself may change, but rarely does so).

More rarely still, a perfect cadence is employed either to lead to an episode at the end of an entry of the subject or else in the course of the episode itself.

403. In any case, a cadence must be employed whenever the musical sense permits it or requires it, just as one uses punctuation in writing. The following examples will illustrate this.

404. From these examples, we shall see that it is not necessary for the subject, after a perfect cadence, to enter in the key, or even the mode of this cadence. The essential point is that the transition should be both natural and logical, and that the music should never suffer by it. Such a result will be easily obtained if the new key has an immediate relationship with the preceding key.

Example:

a) J. S. Bach, Organ Fugue in C major

b) Well-Tempered Clavier, II, Fugue 2

c) **Well-Tempered Clavier, I, Fugue 1**

d) **id. Fugue 4**

405. In (a), the entry of the subject (bar 5) comes on the last note of, and in the key of, the cadence.

In (b), the cadence is on the dominant, in relation to the subject; in (c) and (d), the subject enters in the minor mode immediately after a cadence in the major mode. The study of Bach's fugues will show students, moreover, what great diversity may be brought to the reentries of the subject, so as to avoid monotony and constantly reawaken interest in the fugue.

406. At the École, it is forbidden, after a cadence, to have the subject enter on a dissonance, even a prepared one, as in the following example:[1]

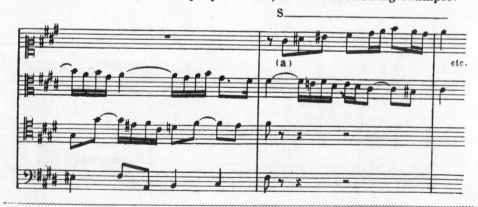

1. This prohibition is applied at the École to all entries of parts. Entries at the École can be made only on consonances.

Fragment (a) in this example would be rectified as shown in (b) in the following way:

or in some similar manner. The subject in this case enters in a key and on a chord foreign to the cadence.

Musically, the first version will always be preferred. The rule that is under consideration here is not plausible. It obviously comes from an erroneous application of the rules of harmony. It is one thing to attack an isolated chord without sufficient preparation; it is another to have a melodic part enter on a dissonance, even though prepared by only a short note, when this part is logically derived from the preceding melody, as is the case in the first example, considered at the École as faulty. On the other hand, from a strictly musical point of view, the second example is not correct since the entry of the subject in the soprano is foreign to what precedes because of a too sudden change of harmony.

407. When the subject begins on the dominant, if one wishes to go to the tonic either directly or with several chords in between, one can often take advantage of the opportunity of having the subject enter at the cadence itself, which is then completed at the moment when the subject uses the tonic or mediant notes:

Example:

J. S. Bach, Fugue for Organ in G minor

408. The preceding method of approach is also applicable to the subject which begins on the dominant followed by the tonic and uses the seventh degree, with the latter considered, in this case, as the third of the dominant chord.

Example:

J. S. Bach,   Fugue for Organ in G major

409. Sometimes, the subject, beginning on the tonic, may be introduced at a perfect cadence terminating an episode. This is especially apt to be done when the episode which follows is based on a figure different from the one which served as main motive for the preceding one.

Example:

J.S. Bach,   Fugue for Organ in C major

In this example, the perfect cadence is avoided by the employment (in the soprano) of a B-flat (at the end of the first bar) which prepares the key of F major in which the subject is to enter. However, the perfect cadence in this key does not end until the 2nd bar of the subject, which enters on the cadential formula itself (bars 4 and 5).

410. The employment of the perfect cadence is also justified in the course of an episode when this episode is continued with a figure different from the one which begins it. Example:

J.S. Bach,   Fugue for Organ in G major

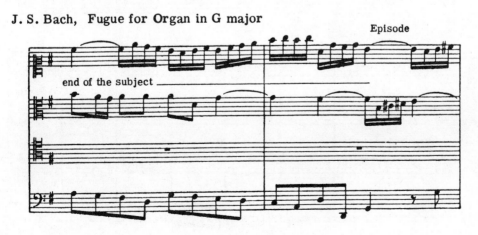

Here the cadence, which has been avoided in the second bar by the suspension on the third beat, comes about halfway in the third bar. Note that it gives very sharp relief to the new melodic figure which serves as main motive for the rest of the episode.

411. With the same reservation not to interrupt the melodic continuity of the fugue, sometimes one employs a perfect cadence to begin an episode at the end of an entry of the subject.

The following example begins and ends on a perfect cadence. Here the employment of these two cadences is justified by the length of the subject and by the deeply expressive nature of its melody which allowed Bach to construct this fugue by continuously creating contrasts in one way or another between the subject and the episodes which enframe it. With this disposition, rarely used in the school fugue, the impression is created of a dialogue full of charm and melancholy.

J. S. Bach,   Fugue for Organ in A major

412. In whatever way a perfect cadence is used in the course of a fugue, it should be introduced only when it is motivated by the melodic sense of the parts. There are some fugues that will have perfect cadences many times in a natural manner; others in which its employment will not be justified. A rule cannot be formulated in this regard. One will acquire increased judgment by analyzing Bach's fugues from this point of view.

The fugue in A major, the source of the preceding example, is an excellent model. Perfect cadences are numerous in it, and, each time, their necessity springs from the expressive nature of the passage which gives rise to them or from the relief which they bring to what follows them.

413. There is, however, one part of the fugue where they should not appear: the exposition. Here, the entries should form an uninterrupted chain, and one should use all one's ingenuity to avoid the slightest lapse of continuity in the melodic thread and in the texture of the parts. The exposition should form an indivisible whole which is complete only upon the completion of the fourth entry of the subject.

414. What is called—quite improperly, by the way—fugue style is nothing but the collection of procedures used to construct a fugue. Just because all fugues have in common the characteristic of being written in an imitative form, it does not follow that all should resemble each other. This is exactly the criticism which we are justified in making of the school fugue: to wish to impose upon every kind of subject a uniform procedure and plan. And one must also be careful not to commit the error of composing the same fugue on subjects that have different styles. Actually, each subject has in itself a special style due as much to the nature and rhythm of its melody as to the medium (vocal or instrumental) used by the composer. This does not have to be illustrated.

Fugue Style.

415. The only differences that can be found between a vocal fugue and an instrumental fugue are due precisely to the necessity, for the one, of keeping in mind the range of the voices and the difficulties of intonation of certain intervals; and, for the other, the conditions of execution.

Therefore, unity of style in a fugue will be assured by the observation of this one precept: Make a fugue out of its subject.

416. The first condition to be fulfilled will, obviously, be to establish for the listener the expressive character of the subject. Except for indications of mode and time signature, which have only a very general, vague value, note that it is precisely upon the countersubject that has fallen the role of spelling out the nature of the subject. If its only purpose were to give the subject a harmonic complement, the countersubject could, without any inconvenience, be replaced by some sort of counterpoint.

Expressive Function of the Countersubject.

The countersubject, therefore, will have to accentuate the character of the subject not only by setting off the rhythm of the subject, but also, and much more so, by bringing out its expressive side.

417. The countersubject—and this has been stated before—should contrast with the subject, but in no case can it be incompatible with it. It is the violation of this principle which makes certain fugues appear insupportable to us because, contrasted with a subject of an austere, noble, and grave nature, is a countersubject that sounds like a technical exercise and moves at a jerky pace that conveys an impression of parody.

Although Bach sometimes falls into this irregularity—albeit more rarely than others; but especially in vocal fugues—it is in instrumental fugues (organ and clavier) of his that the most beautiful models will be found.

418. If we take, for example, the subject of his fugue for organ in E minor,

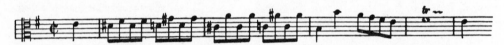

the indications that can be obtained from either the mode or the time signature (barred in ¢) are rather vague. Such a subject, from the point of view of expression, is evidently capable of the most diverse interpretations.

Then, immediately upon the entry of the answer, the countersubject appears,

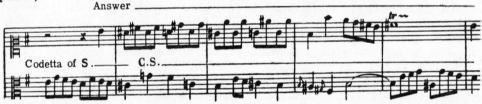

henceforth no further doubt is possible. The countersubject, by its expressive nature, impresses upon the subject an absolutely definitive character, and, as a result, is going to take on a preponderant role in the genesis of the fugue from the point of view of style. For the whole fugue to be the development of the musical idea proposed by the subject as it has been revealed by the countersubject, the latter must take from the subject not simply its rhythms, but, further, its feeling, its expression. New rhythms, even new melodic figures can be introduced from that point on in the course of the fugue, as long as they participate in the expressive nature of subject and countersubject, or else, by contrast, accentuate this nature.

419. Generally speaking, a subject of serious aspect will call for an animated countersubject more readily than will a subject with a light, lively rhythm. In the former case, however, if movement is given to the countersubject, it can be done only with the aid of melodic designs of a very expressive nature, under penalty of falling into the error for which we criticized the fugues above with their technical exercises.

If the subject is lively, it can easily be understood that a countersubject that is too animated would run the risk of bringing confusion into the texture, and the effectiveness of the fugue would be lessened by it.

It is virtually impossible to formulate rules on this particular point, and the examples of countersubjects given in Chapters IV and V, and at the end of the first part of this treatise, as well as the study of the fugues of Bach and of the other masters, will instruct students sufficiently. Thus we may dispense with the task of citing new examples here.

420. Free parts used in the exposition should also contribute to accentuating the nature of the subject. They cannot be conceived as musically indifferent parts or as harmonic fill-ins. From this point of view they are to be considered as countersubjects that cannot be inverted and are, for that very reason, modifiable at will. But in no case should they be in a style that is not in keeping with the style of the subject.

Free Parts.

421. Now it is understood that, with the whole fugue contained in essence in the exposition, unity of style in the exposition will assure unity of style in the fugue. And we can infer that unity of style is synonymous with unity of expression. It will therefore be possible, without violating this unity, to introduce into a fugue new elements, rhythmic or melodic, provided that they do not introduce any modifications in the expressive nature of the fugue and affect only its exterior aspect—the clothing, so to speak, not the body.

Unity of Style. Unity of Expression.

422. If it is most usual in a fugue to construct each episode on a different figure, there are a number of fugues in which all the episodes are built on the same melodic or rhythmic figure. The essential thing, in this case, is to know how, with the help of contrapuntal devices, to present the same melody in different aspects or to know how to create a sufficient number of different melodic figures with the same rhythm.[1]

Examples of this last type of fugue are to be found in Bach, for example: the fugue for organ in D minor in which all the episodes are based on the following motive, presented each time with different combinations:

the 12th fugue of the Well-Tempered Clavier, I, developed entirely with this rhythmic figure:

to cite only two. These will be profitably analyzed from this particular point of view, put into open score. There are, as well, many others which the student can seek out for himself.

423. If unity of style is to become one with unity of expression, it will be necessary to choose with the greatest care the figures destined for the various episodes. This work should be done, remember, as soon as the ex-

Character of the Episodes.

---

1. This is not acceptable at the Conservatory, especially in competitive examinations. It is required—without any reasons being given—that all episodes be constructed on different motives, in direct contradiction not only to the habitual practice of the masters of the fugue, but also to the methods of procedure of symphonic development.

position is terminated. One should first take into account the imitations and other contrapuntal devices to which these figures lend themselves. One should avoid all combinations which might not conform with the nature of the fugue and might weaken its interest because they lack musical character. Then one will set up a melodic plan for the whole fugue, conforming to what was pointed out in Chapter V for the preparation of the episodes, taking care, however, at each entry of the subject, to write the parts in almost their final version in order to bind the episodes together.[1]

424. Although by its very essence melodic invention escapes any exact rule, one can nevertheless call to the attention of students some of the methods of procedure used by masters to make a musical idea stand out more, make its development more spirited and more interesting, and give more melodic unity to the fugue.

One of these procedures consists first of all in treating a melodic idea in a passage, then, having momentarily abandoned it for another figure, in reproducing the same passage, but in another key. As we shall see in the third part of this treatise, this is a method of symphonic development frequently used by Mozart and Beethoven.

We come upon a striking example of this in one of the episodes in the fugue for organ in G minor ("The Great") by J. S. Bach, an episode whose main melodic line may be succinctly presented as follows:

A first passage consisting of two similar figures A+A modulates from

E-flat to B-flat, then from B-flat to F minor; a second passage, with a very short antecedent (b),

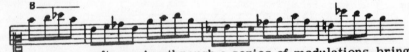

after going through a series of modulations, brings back the first passage, which is reproduced in its entirety, transposed so that its keys are now C minor and G minor. There follows an entry of the subject in the main key of the fugue:

425. It is certain—one can be convinced by analysis—that a large share of the interest in this episode stems from the employment of a theme very simple in itself. However, as ingenious as the disposition of the parts in the realization by Bach may be, one will easily come to realize by eliminating the return of the first passage, that all the élan and glow of this episode— and consequently its expressive value—are due solely to the return of this passage before the entry of the subject.

1. On this subject, see the example given at the end of this volume, Section 505.

Here is the realization by Bach, represented at first in the form of a plan of execution, then, in its exact text, in open score:

426. One must have a certain touch—if one may use the expression—to make use of the preceding method. The subsidiary motives and figures should evoke an interest at least as great as the main theme of the episode. In its new appearance the first passage should have, as much as possible, a different disposition of parts, so as to avoid monotony and repetition. By comparing the above example with the following one, taken from a fugue by Franz Schubert, one will become aware of this fault and thus be able to avoid it:

427. Here, by contrast to what was seen in the example taken from Bach, Section 425, there is no development of the theme; only a simple repetition resulting from the transposition to the fifth below of the first term A of the sequence. This is a repetition, and the impression of monotony and dryness is still further accentuated by the literal reproduction, in the second term of the sequence, of dispositions used in the first term. Since the relationship of the parts is the same, the sonority does not change. Thus, one is left with the feeling, not of an idea that progresses, but rather of a formula which keeps repeating itself—a kind of harmonic progression of pseudo- melodic aspect.

428. The different impression that results from one and the other of these passages is specifically due to the fact that, in the Schubert example there is, properly speaking, no melodic line resulting from the flow of the parts but a series of formulas, while Bach, with a simpler musical structure, has been able to get a true melodic flow, alive and varied.

429. Furthermore, in proportion to the quality of the initial figure, the same harmonic progression will give rise in one case to a series of flat and mournful formulas, in the other, to a melodic line full of life and elegance.

Here, for example, are two episodes: one taken from the fugue by Schubert already cited, the other, from the 13th fugue of the Well—Tempered Clavier, I. Both are constructed according to an identical method (each part imitating itself) and on a similar harmonic progression. The first is nothing but formula; the second is alive and develops a melodic line with a distinct, elegant, firm contour. And yet, the point of departure is the same for both, the methods employed are similar. One can find only a single difference between them: the quality of the musical material employed.

430. The thing that cannot be studied too much in Bach's work is the extreme variety of method—apart from his technical skill—which he uses to bring back the subject either during or after the episodes; and the admirable skill with which, in every case, he makes the most varied elements converge musically in the expressive unity of a fugue.

We have already considered this particular point (Sections 402ff.) in studying the employment of the cadence. We shall illustrate here, with an example from the fugue in E minor for organ, how Bach, in an episode with great depth of feeling, was able to reserve the most expressive part of his melodic line for the reentry of the subject.

I should like to emphasize here, however, that extreme care should be taken to see that the method is intimately linked with the musical idea, forming, so to speak, a unit with it. While I lay one open to examination, take care not to lose sight of the other. In that way I will not have to fall into an esthetic-literary jargon which, when applied to a musical work, can serve only as a kind of pretext for empty, meaningless phraseology. Only music and musical expression can serve as commentary on music; and the best way to convey the feeling of a beautiful musical phrase is to have it played or sung, not written about.

Example:

431. Instead of insisting on the intrinsic beauty of this fragment, a beauty musicians will feel without having to overflow—as a critic would—into lyrical effusions, I shall take the more practical point of view of the musician's craft and shall point out that Bach proceeded by means of a series of contrasts. Thus, he practiced the art of opposition which is too little known to a number of composers. The episode is composed essentially of two progressions, one (A) descending, the other (B) ascending. The latter, **deliberately** anticipating the tonality in which the subject is going to appear, uses the same figure with the same cadence four times in succession, but in different combinations and consequently in different sonorities. This apparent monotony places the entry of the subject in sharper relief. At this moment everything converges to augment the intensity of the expression: the melodic line which, in the scale of pitches, reaches its highest point; the return of subject and counter-subject. The intensity, from that point on, can only decrease progressively, and this attenuation of expressive feeling is continued for two more bars after the subject has finished its entry, while a new episode begins.

432. It is no longer a question here of devices in writing but one of musical composition; and it is at this point that one should remember the principle that a fugue must be composed before it is written. What makes the quality of a fugue, as of any musical work, is not so much the skill with which various contrapuntal devices are manipulated, as it is the value of the ideas for which these methods serve as means of expression.

433. Furthermore, throughout the entire fugue, there must be evidence that it is the work of a musician and composer. From this point of view, each part must be the object of the same painstaking care and the same effort. The stretto especially needs the exercise of judgment and musical sense at every instant. One basic principle should guide the student: "Never—but never—sacrifice music to mere contrapuntal combinations." That is, admit these combinations only insofar as they will produce a musical effect, a melodic flow, and pitilessly reject all others, however ingenious they may be.

434. In the school fugue, there are several ways to link the first part of the fugue with the stretto. One may:
    1. link the last episode directly to the first stretto;
    2. have a deceptive cadence, with a suspension, marked by a pedal point between the episode and the stretto;
    3. use a pedal on the dominant (or more rarely on another degree) before the stretto, joining this pedal point directly with the stretto without interruption, or else separating it from the stretto.

Various Linkings of the Stretto.

435. Whatever disposition may be adopted, the last episode should prepare the stretto by a more closely-knit structure, so that the stretto is the natural, logical continuation of the first part of the fugue without one's getting the impression of a repetition of the exposition or of an interruption in the musical sense.

436. In Chapter IX, we examined in some detail the various aspects which a pedal may take. What we said about it makes it easy to realize its function in the musical composition of a fugue. Harmonically, the pedal has the advantage of making it possible to group the most distant chords over a tonal degree of the main key and of allowing them to succeed each other rapidly without sacrificing any feeling for tonality. In the same way, melodically, it can pull together the main motives of the fugue even if they appear in distant keys. As a result, it makes it possible to bring a new _élan_ to the fugue at the very moment when it approaches its conclusion.

Role of the Pedal.

437. Moreover, it is near this conclusion that the pedal logically finds its place—that is, either before the stretto, which is like the peroration of the fugue, or at the end of this peroration. The choice obviously depends on whether the heightening of the tonal sense is brought about by a pedal point on the tonic—an affirmation of the main key—or by a pedal point on the dominant. The latter brings about, because of the prolonged duration of this degree, the irresistible need for a perfect cadence. The need for a pedal near the conclusion exists even though, in the second section of the fugue, there is

Place of the Pedal.

a pedal on another degree than the dominant or tonic. This degree assumes, in relation to the tonalities used immediately before or after it, the nature of a dominant—never a tonic, which would necessarily imply the idea and feeling of a conclusion.

438. It can now be seen that it is impossible to introduce the tonic pedal before the place assigned to it logically, that is, at the extreme end of the stretto, whether the fugue ends on this pedal, or whether—and this is less frequent—the pedal point is followed by a final cadence, perfect or plagal.

439. The above explanations have been given to justify, in theory and with reasons drawn from the very nature of the pedal, the place that it has in the fugue. It now remains to examine the importance of the pedal and the different ways in which it may be conceived and realized from the point of view of musical composition.

Importance of the Pedal.   440. The importance of the pedal—that is, its length and its musical quality—varies for many reasons. With the masters, there are a number of fugues in which the pedal is not employed. In other cases, one or more pedals are found, some very short, not more than two bars in length, others very much extended, sometimes seeming excessively so, in relation to the length of the fugue of which they are part. But this is a matter of judgment on the part of the composer. The main thing is never to give an impression of lack of proportion. What does the actual length of such or such part of the fugue really mean if it does not seem long when it is heard?

441. In the school fugue, it is the rule to use either a pedal point on the dominant, or on the tonic, or, at the wish or the student, both. The assigned places are: (1) The pedal point on the dominant comes at the end of the episode immediately preceding the first stretto. In this case, a tonic pedal point is used at the end of the fugue. (2) A pedal point on the dominant comes in the last part of the stretto and is followed by a short tonic pedal point as a conclusion. In the latter case, certain professors prefer that the two pedal points not be immediately linked, but that they be separated by one or two bars of stretto. Others show a preference for a direct linking using a deceptive cadence, following a formula often practiced in harmony lessons. That is all a matter of individual preference and does not constitute a rule, but, on the other hand, only a kind of fashion, varying according to the seasons and the directors. I am setting this down only for the record, leaving it up to the student to judge the path to follow when he has to take tests and examinations. This has nothing at all to do with the study of fugue. I will point out, however, that on those rare occasions when their fugues approach the form of the school fugue, the masters have employed the pedal point on the dominant before the stretto, saving the tonic pedal point for the end of the fugue.

442. Since the musical elements used to construct a pedal vary according to whether this pedal is used before the first stretto or at the end of   the

last, it is obvious that in each of these cases the musical composition of the pedal will be different.

Although all this belongs to the domain of the imagination and although exact rules cannot be formulated on the subject of musical invention, nevertheless, I shall point out to students several methods of procedure which will serve as a basis for practice in their first efforts and will ultimately enable them to create new forms more easily.

443. The pedal, most often, enters during the course of an episode. It thus contributes to the continuation of the episode. To facilitate our study, we will assume that this entry, in the largest number of cases, can come at one of the three following points—remembering first of all that we are concerned with a pedal point on the dominant used before the first stretto:

Composition of the Pedal.

1. When the episode has reached the high point of an ascending melodic line;

2. When the episode has reached the low point of a descending melodic line;

3. When the episode has not reached its extreme point in the course of a melodic movement, either ascending or descending.

I repeat: this method of generalizing is in itself too restricted and serves no other purpose than to give students a definite point of departure for their exercises.

444. In the first two cases, when the high or low point of the melodic line has been reached, the logical thing to do is to continue the episode over the pedal, with the melodic line turning the other way. The musical materials should remain the same. This is stated as a principle but not as an exact rule.

Example:

a) Pedal entering in the course of an episode at the high point of an ascending line.

b) Pedal entering at the low point of a descending line in the course of an episode.

Max d'Ollone, Fugue on a subject by Gounod

445. When the pedal enters in an episode during the course of an ascending or descending line, it is natural for the line not to be interrupted and for it to continue over the pedal, to turn afterwards as soon as its high or low point has been reached. Here is an example of the form that this part of the fugue can take in such a case:[1]

J. Boulay, Contest Fugue (First Prize, 1897) on a subject by Th. Dubois

Episode

1. The method employed in this example can be applied in the same way to the construction of an episode in which the pedal enters during the course of an ascending line. This can be very easily understood and does not require that we give a second example.

446. These are the three ways of introducing a pedal during the course of an episode. I advise students at first to follow the pattern of the models given. Afterwards, they will be able to bring more variety to their procedures, which, as may easily be imagined, can have many different applications. However, they ought not forget that if rigidity must be avoided in composition, so must working without an established plan be avoided. At the École, disorganization, no matter how fine it may be, is never effective in art.

Examples of Linkings of the Stretto.

447. The linking of the second section of the fugue with the stretto can be done, at the will of the composer, in varied ways. It has already been seen in preceding examples. From this particular viewpoint, here are some more models to be analyzed. Given a free hand, students can create similar ones, remaining, however, within the limits set by logic and a feeling for proportion.

a) **Ch. Koechlin,   Fugue on a subject by A. Gedalge**

1st Stretto.

b) **Max d'Ollone,   Fugue on a subject by Massenet**

c) Henri Rabaud,   Fugue on a subject by Massenet

1st Stretto.

d) Fernand Halphen,   Fugue on a subject by A. Gedalge

a Tempo.

e) A. Savard,   Fugue on a Subject by Massenet

448. If a pedal is not used before the first stretto, the preceding episode can nevertheless be linked with the stretto by a method similar to one of those enumerated above; the pedal is actually only incidental in the episode, and, if it influences the episode from the harmonic point of view by allowing a more varied and freer flow of parts, its omission will not relieve the student of his obligation to give this last episode the compact form that the approach of the stretto requires.[1]

449. In a case such as the above, it is a good idea to have an entry of the subject in the dominant or the subdominant, or even in the main key[2] shortly before the first stretto, as the masters have often done. Here is a convincing example from the fugue for organ in G major by J. S. Bach:

---

1. There is more to be said: When a subject lends itself to so many canonic combinations that all cannot be used in the stretto without its becoming too long, it is permissible to use the least compact of these combinations either in the two episodes preceding the stretto or even in some other place. One will not be reproached for anticipating the stretto.

2. In such a case, it is permissible to change the main key from major to minor, and vice versa. This method gives more relief to the entry of the stretto, where the subject enters in the true mode of the fugue. The following example is an illustration.

Subject at the 2nd degree of the main key

450. The preceding example has been quoted at some length in order to show how, with the entry of the subject at the second degree, the writing of the parts has already become more compact and progressively approaches the character of the stretto. The episode, a canonic one based on a fragment of the subject, is closely linked by the bass figure to those figures used immediately before, in close imitations, in the three lower parts. Note also that the main motive of the episode, first stated by the tenor in the fifth bar of the example, is always presented so that the melodic line which is going to end (eighth bar) upon the entry of the subject is readily perceptible and stands out as much as possible.

451. This line should be an essential characteristic of the stretto, to avoid an effect of confusion. By definition, a stretto is a series of entries of the subject and answer brought closer and closer together. These entries must be combined so that, in their entirety, they give the impression of an uninterrupted melodic line, and not just a series of melodic fragments, disconnected and simply juxtaposed, like some sort of composition with compartments, or drawers, if one may use the expression. Its least fault would be incoherence, and its worst would be monotony due to a more and more rapid repetition of the same formula, the head of the subject.

Melodic Line of the Stretto.

452. To arrive at the desired result, it would be helpful to conceive an overall plan for the stretto, a plan similar to the one I indicated for the first part of the fugue. If the stretto is sufficiently extended, it can be considered on a basis of successive periods of certain dimensions. What must be avoided at all costs is to let the stretto drift along at the mercy of its combinations and subsequently wind up incoherently. It is the same with the fugue as with a building in which the details contribute to the overall line, without altering it, from whatever angle one may stand to look at it.

453. One should take into account this characteristic of the stretto by putting into open score and analyzing several of the fugues of the Well- Tempered Clavier by Bach, especially those numbered I: 1, 4, 8, 20, 22; II: 3, 5, 9, 22. Since composition of the stretto in the school fugue does not have as narrow restrictions as the first two sections of the fugue, it is easy for students to get closer to Bach's forms. With this reservation, however: Do not borrow certain styles of writing considered in high places as too free. Nevertheless, I advise students to study closely these so-called licenses, which almost always have an artistic raison d'etre. From every point of view, this analysis cannot help but be profitable to them, for something is always to be gained from mingling with well-bred people.

Tonic Pedal.

454. The methods of composition that I have indicated for the dominant pedal point used before the stretto also apply to pedals on the dominant and on the tonic when they are employed at the end of the fugue. The only difference comes from the musical material used. The writing of the parts, in this last case, should always be in the character of the stretto. One should refer to the examples given above (Chapters IX and XI).

Conclusion
of the Fugue.

455. The conclusion proper of the fugue is made on a tonic pedal or immediately afterward. In any case it is made with a perfect or plagal cadence. Here again, no rule. Everything is left to the invention of the student. The one recommendation to be made is not to lengthen the conclusion needlessly. The student should not hesitate to sacrifice a few combinations, useless if their only purpose is length, but he should not give the opposite impression either: that he is interrupting when he still has something to say. Just as it is necessary to continue, so is it necessary to stop at the right point. If there is one part of the fugue to which the poet's _est modus in rebus_ applies, it is the conclusion.[1]

---

1. In the fugues cited at the end of this volume are examples of strettos with these various combinations. One may also refer to Chapters IX and X, in which are suggested several models, with or without the tonic pedal.

CHAPTER XIII

The Introduction of a New Subject and the Modifications Which a Subject Can Undergo In the Course of a Fugue

456. Up to this point we have considered the fugue as a musical composition developed exclusively from elements taken from the exposition. However, in the works of the masters, one frequently encounters fugues in which, at some point, new melodic ideas are introduced. These ideas are foreign to the subject, the countersubject, or the free parts employed at the beginning. These new figures are not introduced arbitrarily. Their purpose is to augment interest in the fugue as much by the contrast they present with the subject as by the combinations which they can form with it.

457. So as not to harm the expressive unity, each new figure introduced in the fugue must have a style similar to that of the subject. That does not imply that it should resemble the subject. Quite the contrary. It should contrast with it, but the contrast should not be an incongruous one, even though the new figure has a sharply individual character in its rhythm and melody. From this contrast itself there will inevitably result a renewed interest in the entire composition.

Definition of the New Subject.

458. A melodic or rhythmic figure used under these conditions is given the name of new subject. This new subject should be written in invertible counterpoint with at least the main subject and, if possible, with the countersubject of the main subject. The new subject should also be accompanied by a countersubject, which may or may not be invertible with the main subject and its countersubject. In any case the new subject should be conceived in such a way that the emphasis is always reserved for the main subject, the very foundation of the fugue. Any infraction of this rule would obviously be at the risk of subverting the musical sense of the fugue if the introduction of the new subject has resulted in bringing in developments completely foreign to the beginning of the work or even simply too different from it. Therefore, from this arises the necessity of attributing to the new subject an importance only secondary in its general character and of subordinating it to the main subject and the needs of its countersubject. It confines itself to combining

Characteristics of the New Subject.

with them in invertible counterpoint in two, three, or four parts, as the case may be.

459. It follows therefore that the composition of a new subject simply means creating, with respect to the main subject, a supplementary countersubject which will be used in the fugue only after a certain point. Likewise, if the new subject is itself accompanied by a countersubject, one considers that, in actuality, there will be simply one more countersubject for the main subject.

However, a distinction of an exclusively musical order must be made between a simple countersubject and a new subject. The new subject should have a more individual and a more clear-cut physiognomy than a countersubject.[1] From this point of view, it will even be useful, sometimes, to give it more length than the main subject, as we shall presently see.

Place of the New Subject.

460. Generally, in the school fugue, the new subject is used after the second episode, either in one of the keys related to the main key, or in this key itself. To set it off in sharp relief, it may be preceded by a cadence in the dominant of the key in which it is going to enter. One then proceeds with an exposition of the new subject identical to the one which was made of the main subject at the beginning of the fugue.

461. The new subject may be accompanied by a suitable countersubject, or, lacking this, by the countersubject of the main subject. But it is a good idea not to use the main subject before at least the fourth entry of the new subject. From this point on, the fugue follows its course until its termination using the main subject and the new subject simultaneously with, if they are called for, countersubjects. All the subsequent developments are taken from these themes.

Order of Modulations.

462. Here, as a guide, is a suggested order of modulations in a school fugue in which a new subject has been introduced. Students are free to make other dispositions if it suits them:
a. Exposition;
b. Episode;
c. Counter exposition (not required);
d. Episode;
e. Subject in the relative minor key (or relative major key, depending on the mode of the subject);
f. Episode and pause on the dominant of the main key;
g. Exposition of the new subject (in the main key);
h. Episode based on the new subject;
i. New subject and main subject combined at the second degree (or at the sixth degree if the main mode of the fugue is minor).

---

1. The new subject, like the main subject, must constitute a complete melodic entity.

j. Answers of the new subject and the main subject combined;

k. Episode based on elements of the new subject and main subject combined;

l. New subject and main subject combined, at the subdominant;

m. Episode based on elements taken from the two subjects with a dominant pedal;

n. Stretto.

One may omit the answers indicated in (j) and pass on to (l) with a short episode.

463. It is to be understood that the order of modulations may be varied. For example, after the exposition (or counter exposition, if there is one) an episode may be introduced leading to an entry of the main subject in the subdominant key; then, with the help of a short episode, the answer can enter in the key of the second degree (assuming the main key of the fugue to be major). A new episode leads to a cadence on the dominant of the relative minor where the new subject enters, etc.

464. The stretto may have the following structure, allowing each one the freedom to proceed according to his will, guiding himself by the nature of the subjects and their projected combinations: *Structure of the Stretto.*

a. First stretto of the main subject;

b. Stretto of the new subject;

c. Combined strettos of the two subjects, of varying number, the general structure to be the same as with any simple stretto.

465. Here are several examples by Bach illustrating a new subject against the main subject. Students will be able to refer to the fugues cited and study them.

a) J. S. Bach, Fugue for Organ in F major

b) J. S. Bach, Fugue for Organ in C minor

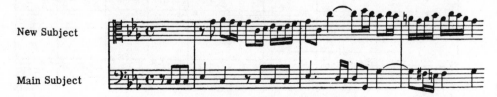

Note that, in this example, with the mutation in the answer of the main subject, there is a corresponding mutation in the answer of the new subject:

Answer of the
New Subject

Answer of the
Main Subject

c) J. S. Bach, The Art of Fugue

Main Subject

Countersubject
of the New Subject

New Subject

In this last example the new subject and its countersubject begin and end before the main subject. Thus they stand out much more than otherwise, and cannot be mistaken for simple countersubjects of the main subject.

Working Out the New Subject.

466. When a new subject is to be used in a fugue, it is useful to work it out in advance, that is, at the same time as one works out the countersubject of the main subject. Their combination will then require the use of invertible counterpoint in three parts. If the new subject is accompanied by a countersubject that can be inverted simultaneously with the main subject and its countersubject, they are combined in invertible counterpoint in four parts. In short, as I have already said, it comes down to getting out of a subject three different, invertible countersubjects. The first one is begun one or two bars before the beginning of the main subject and has the figures with the most character; it is selected as the new subject. But the other two countersubjects should always be shorter than the main subject.

Analysis of a Fugue with Two Subjects.

467. Here, beginning with the exposition, is an analysis of the last fugue of Bach's Art of Fugue, in which two new subjects are used in succession:

J. S. Bach, The Art of Fugue, Contrapunctus XIX

Allegro moderato e maestoso.

Exposition.

This exposition does not include a countersubject in the strict sense of the word. Note, however, that the two free parts that accompany the subject from the 13th bar on are reproduced almost exactly with the fourth entry of the answer. Note also the tonal unity of this exposition: The subject and answer remain entirely in the key of D minor, except for bars 15, 16, and 17 in which the keys of G minor and A minor are used.

468. The entire development that follows the exposition of the main subject is treated, not in accordance with the principles of the school fugue, but in the form of strettos alternately direct and by inversion, with the entries occurring at varying distances. The motives of the episodes of this first part have been taken from the counterpoints which take the place of counter-subjects in the exposition.

Reversed Canonic Stretto in Inversion

Canonic Stretto (reversed)

EPISODE I

(built on a figure taken from the exposition 8th bar)

469. In the 114th bar there begins the exposition of the first new subject. This exposition is preceded by a short pedal on the dominant of the main key, and it is in this key and at the cadence itself that the entry of the new subject is made. This subject, in its rhythm, its fresh melodic character, and its length, differs essentially from the main subject.[1] The exposition, which is regular, ends with the 140th bar. It is followed by an episode of six bars, partly canonic, constructed on the two figures used in bar 126. In the 147th bar, the new subject reappears in the main key, this time in the soprano, and, starting with the following bar, combined with the main subject in the bass. A very short episode, constructed on the same figures as the preceding one, modulates to the dominant, and the same combination of new subject and main subject reappears in the alto and tenor parts. A new episode (bars 162 to 167) is followed by a different combination of the two subjects, with the main subject this time not entering until the third bar of the new subject.

After the eighth episode, the new subject returns in the subdominant key, and while it is thus being heard in the bass, a canonic stretto of the main subject and answer appears, beginning in bar 182, and is linked to an episode which ends in bar 193 with a perfect cadence in the key of G minor (subdominant of the main key).

Exposition of a First New Subject.

---

1. This first new subject is longer than the main subject. Its length has the advantage of differentiating it better from a simple countersubject, which, in every case, should be shorter than the main subject. In this fugue, since the main subject does not have any countersubject, it was necessary to give more importance to the new subject by making it longer, in order to avoid confusion of this kind.

Note also that the entries of the main subject against the new subject occur at varying distances from the head of the new subject. Thus, there is renewed interest at each entry.

Exposition of the 1st New Subject

EPISODE VIII

470. Immediately after the cadence, the exposition of the second new subject begins. Its first four notes spell the name "Bach" with the letters of the alphabet used for German pitch-names. The exposition of this new subject is in the form of a stretto between the new subject and its answer, with the answer entering before the second new subject has completed its entry.

471. In bar 198, the tenor takes up a figure already used as a free countersubject in the exposition of the main subject (bars 8, 15, 20) and one which has served for the episodes of the first part of the fugue. After an episode based on this same figure, the second new subject enters in the tenor, followed by an entry in the alto in inversion in the bar before the last. Immediately thereafter, there begins a compact stretto (at a distance of a half bar) of the second new subject and its answer slightly modified (bar 220) in its ending. The bass then takes up again, without interruption, (bar 222) the second new subject in inversion. The alto has it again in direct motion (bar 227) in the key of the subdominant, while other figures recalling the first new subject appear in the free parts. A short episode, built upon these same figures, ends in a cadence on the dominant of the main key.

472. Note that the answer of this second new subject is not regular. This fact is of no importance for the case in point. In the strictest school fugue one may proceed in this way and even have an answer to the new subject at whatever interval one may wish.

Note also that this entire part of the fugue keeps almost constantly to the two keys of the first and fourth degrees of the main key of the fugue. There is no rule for this. Students are left every liberty in this respect. It is a good idea, however, to note that limited modulation is to be preferred.

Exposition of the 2nd new subject

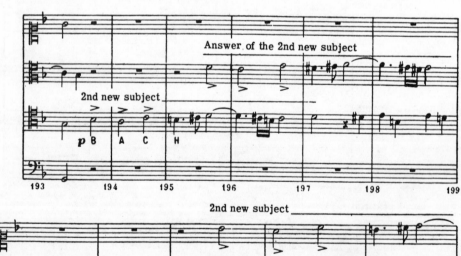

EPISODE X

Combination of the Three Subjects.

473. The last part of the fugue begins here. Bach has written only six complete bars of it; the seventh is simply outlined. This last part should contain all the combinations that he intended to make with the three subjects used in succession. It would be rather presumptuous to try to finish such a work. Nevertheless, I do think it would be useful for the student to attempt to write the end of this fugue and to approach as closely as possible the inimitable model left by Bach.

Combination of the three subjects

474. In studying this fugue one will find that the new subject allows the introduction into the fugue of elements very different from the main subject and countersubject at a time when the expressive character of the piece has been quite definitely established by developments already based on the main subject and countersubject. As a result, introduction of new figures cannot harm the overall unity. It is for this reason also that the new subject should have, even more than a simple countersubject, a well-defined character and should form a melodic unit. In a word, it is necessary for a new subject to be a musical phrase with a complete meaning, just as the main subject or countersubject is.

475. It is obvious that no school fugue could possibly reach a stage of development comparable to that of the one studied above. Students should see in it only a model in which most of the combinations that can be used in a fugue with several subjects are set forth.

476. Generally speaking, what may be extracted from the preceding a-nalyses can be summarized in the following outline for a fugue with two or three subjects:

1. Exposition and development of the first subject;
2. Exposition and development of the second subject;
3. Combination of the two subjects, and final development of the fugue on the basis of this combination.

477. In addition to the introduction of a new subject, the fugue may be further diversified by means of various modifications in the main subject itself or in its countersubject.   **Modifications of a Subject.**

These modifications may bear on the rhythm of the subject or, much more rarely, on its melodic line, which, in any case, should not be altered to the point where it becomes unrecognizable.

Several suggestions are given below. Students will find numerous ex-amples to guide them on this point in the fugues of Bach, Handel, Mozart, and Mendelssohn.

**Modifications
in Rhythm.**

478. In Fugue 6 of the Well-Tempered Clavier, II, the subject

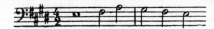

is, at one point, presented in this form, rhythmically modified

and treated in this manner (bars 23 ff.)

479. The Art of Fugue by Bach offers several examples of these trans-
formations of a subject, all of which can be utilized in the school fugue,
Example:

Original subject

**Modifications
in the Length
of the Subject.**

480. In addition to these modifications in rhythm, the subject may, in
the course of the fugue, be used only in part; that is, it may be interrupted
either for the entry of the answer or for the purpose of beginning an episode.

This interruption should occur only on the last part of the subject and
should be as limited as possible. It may in no case affect the head of the
subject. Besides, this procedure is followed only with subjects that are rath-

er long, since there is no reason to use it for short subjects.

481. The initial note of the subject may also be modified in its length. **Initial Note**
When, for example, a subject begins in this manner: **Modified.**

or in a similar manner, it may be presented at a given point thus

or, more rarely:

One must be guided by the requirements of the texture or of the musical
sense, which alone should determine such changes: as, for example, for harmonic reasons the subject may not be able to enter with its initial note in its
original time-value, or perhaps the entry of the subject acquires more emphasis by means of such a modification.

482. In any case, these various changes cannot be employed in the expo- **Final Note of**
sition. The only modification that can be made in the subject in the exposi- **the Subject**
tion, is in its final note, which, starting with the second entry only–and never **Modified in**
with the first entry–may be delayed by a suspension. **the Exposi-**
tion.

Example:

Mendelssohn, Organ fugue

The same observation may be applied to the countersubject.

483. After the first entry of the subject, one may also for purely musical **Modifications**
reasons modify the last note of the answer, so as to link it better with the **in the**
episode or with a new entry of the subject by replacing a minor interval with **Answer.**
a major one, as is illustrated in the following example:

Note that the opposite is hardly admissible. One can see why without my having to explain it.

484. We have at this point terminated the study of those different elements which make up the school fugue. To conclude, we shall review rapidly everything that has been covered; and we shall consider what is, in actual practice, the most rational way to proceed in order to incorporate these various elements into the fugue. This will be the object of the last chapter of this volume.

It is a good idea to note that all the ideas that precede and all those that follow refer to a fugue in four voices. I did not consider it necessary to formulate special rules for fugues in two and three parts, since the writing for two and three voices is naturally derived from the writing for four voices. For the exposition of the fugue alone was it useful to give models in two or three parts. Students will have no difficulty in applying the rules for a fugue in four parts to fugues written for a lesser number of voices.

CHAPTER XIV

Order and Method of Procedure in the Writing of a Fugue. General Summary

485. Once the subject has been selected, here is the procedure one should follow in writing a fugue:

1. Write the answer;

2. Choose the one or more countersubjects, and, if called for, a new subject and its countersubject;

3. Establish the various strettos and canons that can be provided by the subject, answer, countersubjects, and the new subject singly or in combinations;

4. Write the exposition;

5. Choose the melodic elements for each episode and establish the harmonic and melodic plan of the fugue to its conclusion;

6. Write the strettos;

7. Write the part between the exposition and the first stretto in final form.

When a new subject is to be introduced, its entire exposition must be written, establishing the melodic plan of the fugue as above in 5.

486. Point 1. Writing the answer.

1. First of all, harmonize the subject in a natural manner—remembering that from the special point of view of the answer, the dominant of the subject when used in its first melodic movement or at its end, should always be considered as the first degree of the dominant key;

2. In case of alternatives, take as the answer the one that, while satisfying the rule, resembles the melody of the subject the most closely after the necessary mutations.

3. Be sure to number the degree of the scale of the tonic key (or dominant, as the case may be) of each note of the subject. Then answer, degree by degree, in the scale of the dominant when the subject remains in the main key, and in the scale of the tonic when the subject has modulated to the dominant key.

Countersubject.

487. Point 2. Choose the countersubject and new subject (if one is needed).

1. First of all, determine exactly the roots of the harmonies of the subject;

2. Using this harmony, take for the framework of the countersubject the best of the notes invertible with the subject. Do not forget that subject and countersubject should be able to provide each other mutually with a good harmonic bass;

3. Use suspensions as much as possible;

4. Give the countersubject an individual pace and character, different from that of the subject. The countersubject should never imitate the slightest fragment of the subject. Remember that the function of the countersubject is above all to establish the expressive character of the subject. It should therefore be in the same style as the subject, while differing from it melodically and rhythmically. Like the subject, it should form a precise and finished melodic phrase;

5. Never write the countersubject on the answer when the subject is tonal;

6. Verify whether or not the countersubject can harmonize with the answer.

New Subject.

488. The new subject should meet the same qualifications as the countersubjects. It should begin slightly before the subject, which should have the same relation to it as the countersubject has to the main subject.

The new subject is written in invertible counterpoint with either the subject or the countersubject, or with both of them. It itself may be accompanied by a countersubject that can be inverted with the main subject or with the main countersubject, or with both of them.

489. The new subject, therefore, may be combined with and be invertible with:

1. The first subject;
2. The first countersubject;
3. A new countersubject;
4. A new countersubject and the main countersubject;
5. A new countersubject and the first subject;
6. A new countersubject, the first subject, and the first countersubject.

490. Point 3. Establish the various strettos and canons.

1. Look for canons of the subject with itself or with the answer at all intervals;

2. Follow the same procedure for the countersubjects and the new subject;

3. In the same way establish the double canons of the subject with the countersubjects; of the subject with the new subject or its countersubject; of the main countersubject with the new subject; of the new subject and its answer with its countersubject;

4. If the subject does not give canonic strettos, establish the artificial strettos (that is, strettos in which the subject must be interrupted to use the answer). In this case, one must bring into the part that continues the subject, several melodic ideas from the subject;

5. Look for combinations, canonic or otherwise, of subject and countersubjects with the new subject in augmentation and diminution with or without the employment of inversion, retrograde, or retrograde inversion.

491. Point 4. Write the exposition.

1. Always set the subject and countersubject in relief by giving less importance to the free parts;

2. To do that, avoid too many notes or incongruous designs. However, it is a good idea to remember that each figure used in the exposition may have an influence on the ultimate development of the fugue, as much from the point of view of rhythm as from its melodic and expressive character;

3. A short episode may be interpolated between the second and third entries of the subject in order to introduce a rhythmic or melodic figure foreign to subject and countersubject, but in keeping with the nature and style of both of them. Henceforth, one must introduce such elements only in the free parts;

4. Each of the four voices must use, in succession, subject or answer;

5. When the answer cannot enter on the last note of the subject, or, inversely, when the subject cannot enter on the last note of the answer, a short codetta is written to bring back one or the other, as the case may be;

6. The subject or answer must enter as soon as possible after the preceding entry is terminated. But one must avoid, in the exposition, beginning

the answer on a weak beat if the subject begins on a strong one, and vice versa, except in a case where the rhythmic or melodic nature of the subject is not altered by this modification.

7. The exposition of a fugue should establish the main tonality; that is, it should move only between the two keys of the tonic and dominant of the subject;

8. A perfect cadence must not be used in the exposition; nor should it be used to lead to the episode that follows the exposition.

Plan of the Fugue.

492. Point 5. Sketch the plan of the fugue.

1. Separate the subject and countersubject into melodic and rhythmic fragments, just as a melodic phrase is divided up into its constituent motives;

2. The head of the subject and countersubject should not be used before the stretto;

3. Combine with each other melodically the various melodic or rhythmic figures taken from the subject, countersubject, free parts, and new subject (if there is one);

4. Reject those figures which would not stand out sufficiently in a musical context;

5. Look for combinations (canons, various imitations) at every interval to which the selected figures lend themselves. Group them methodically so as to utilize them successively, using as a guide their degree of interest and the closeness of the imitations to which they give rise;

6. For each one of the figures write a natural harmonic bass, with which a harmonic progression can be created that modulates in a logical manner to the related keys;

7. Limit ahead of time the number of modifications of rhythm and melody that each figure will have to submit to, and do the same for the subject, countersubject, and new subject;

8. Once this procedure has been completed, draw up a melodic outline of each episode, making sure of its adaptability to a four-part harmonization. This will not be difficult if the bass has been written carefully so as to establish a logical harmonic progression;

9. Separate the episodes from the parts of the fugue where there are entries of subject and answer. The entries should be written in their final form leaving only the episodes in sketch. The places where the episodes are linked to other parts of the fugue should be worked out.

493. Point 6. Write the strettos.

1. The ensemble structure of the stretto is built of the combinations which were established at the very beginning, when the general plan of the part that follows the exposition was established;

2. Only the first and last strettos should consist of four entries. The others should have only two.

3. In the course of a stretto, one may make transitory modulations to the various related keys, but it is a good idea to come back often to the main key. In any case, the true strettos (subject and answer) as well as the first and last strettos, should be in the main key.

4. The first stretto must not be too much like the exposition of the fugue. To avoid similarity, it is a good idea to space the entries close together and to keep the overall tonality of the stretto in the main key. The free parts used with the answer as well as with the subject should establish harmonies belonging to the main key;

5. The stretto usually ends on a tonic pedal which may be preceded by a pedal on the dominant (or more rarely on another degree).

494. In the course of the fugue, perfect cadences may be used, except in the exposition. They may come either at the end, the beginning, or, more rarely, during the course of an episode. However, cadences should never cause all the parts to stop at the same time.

495. A part should never drop out indiscriminately; that is, taken by itself, before its melodic sense is completed. When it stops, it should always stop so that, taken alone, it implies a cadential harmony.

496. From the flow of the parts there should result an impression of a very clearly defined, overall, melodic line. All the parts, furthermore, should be treated in an exclusively melodic manner, and the melody of the highest part should stand out clearly.

497. As the fugue moves naturally toward its conclusion, each episode should become more compact at its termination than at its beginning. Likewise, the texture should become more and more compact as one nears the stretto.

498. Whenever a subject lends itself to such a large number of canonic combinations that they cannot all be used in the stretto without giving it an unusual length, it is permissible to use subject and answer in stretto in the various tonalities through which the first two sections of the fugue modulate. For this purpose, the least compact of the combinations may be used.

Entries.

499. Each entry should be used to propose the subject, the answer, or an imitative figure, and never merely to fill in the harmony.

Each entry should be preceded, if at all possible, by a rather prolonged rest in whatever part it is going to appear, in order to stand out as clearly as possible.

Two successive entries of subject and answer must not be made in the same voice.

Two successive groups of entries in different keys should not come about in the same order of parts.

Conclusion
of the Fugue.

500. When interest in the fugue is gone, the conclusion should not be unnecessarily prolonged. Neither should the conclusion, on the feeble justification of having a few pleasant or contrived harmonies, be of a nature foreign to what has gone before.

501. Above all, the character of a fugue must arise from its subject and not be the same with subjects that have different styles and natures.

502. It is the expressiveness, and not the agitation or rapidity with which notes follow each other that gives spirit and vehemence to the idea.

503. The following must always be kept in mind:

A fugue—even in academic dress—is a piece of music.

Time spent studying fugue solely from the point of view of contrapuntal combinations is time lost.

Practice in fugal composition is profitable only on the condition that the the art of developing a musical idea is being sought.

This is what I shall try to illustrate in the rest of this work.

504. Before giving examples of entire fugues, I think it is a good idea to show students how—once the exposition is ended and the various elements analyzed and gotten out of the way—a general plan may be set up that embraces the overall structure of the fugue. This will let them see the melodic and harmonic plan at a glance.

Since the elements of this structure have been studied in succession during the first part of this treatise, it will now be useful to collect and summarize the indications scattered throughout the various chapters studied up to this point and apply them to the preparation of a fugue.

The procedure shown in the following example is recommended to students. It will facilitate their task and permit them to marshall their ideas more logically. By avoiding unusual length and repetition, it will show them how to give their fugues better proportions.

505. Overall plan for the composition of a fugue:
1. Melodic and harmonic plan;
2. Plan of execution;
3. Realization.

Note: It is assumed that all the work involved in the finding of counter-subjects, strettos, and canons, and the analysis of the exposition for the choice of motives in the episodes, has been done previously, in accordance with the instructions given in the course of this treatise.

(The numbers placed in front of the various fragments serving as main motives for episodes refer to corresponding numbers placed under the same fragments in the exposition.)

EXPOSITION   Subject by A. Gedalge

Elements
of
EPISODE II

A) Main Motive
2nd countersubject (7)

B) Secondary Motive
end of C.S. 1 (4)

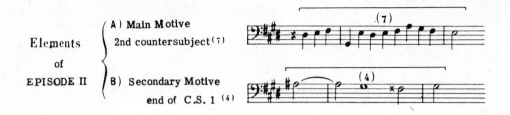

EPISODE II

Melodic and
harmonic plan
of
EPISODE II

Plan
of EXECUTION

REALISATION

Key of the subdominant
Subject

284

Elements
of
EPISODE III

A) **Main Motive**
fragment of C.S. 1 (3)
& codetta of the subj. (2)

B) **Secondary Motive**
fragment of C.S. 2
in inversion

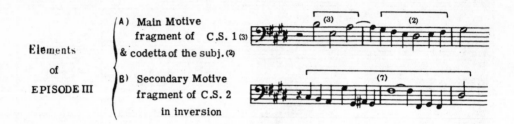

EPISODE III   (canoniq)

Melodic and
harmonic plan
of
EPISODE III

Plan
of EXECUTION

REALISATION

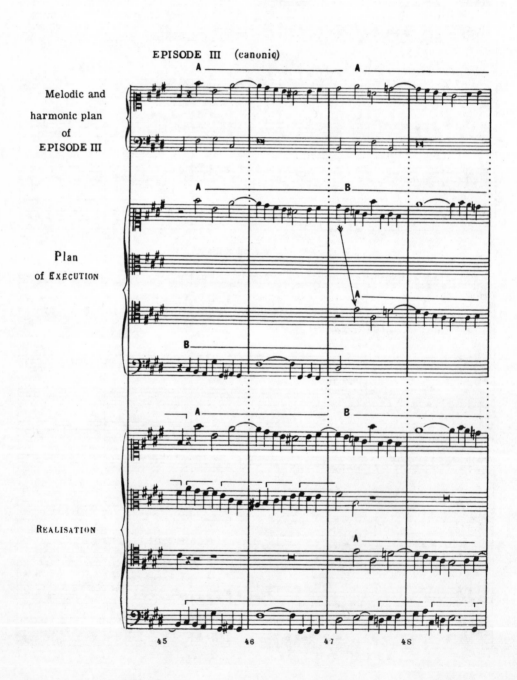

286

288

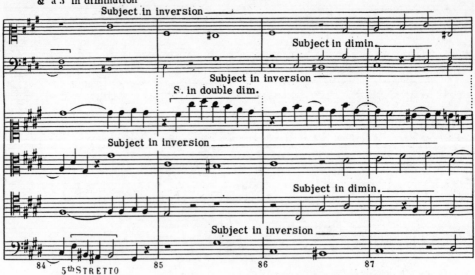

4th STRETTO (in the tonic key)
Canon of the S. à 2 in inversion
& à 3 in diminution

Subject in inversion _____

Subject in dimin. _____

Subject in inversion _____
S. in double dim.

Subject in inversion _____

Subject in dimin. _____

Subject in inversion _____

84   5th STRETTO   85   86   87

in the form of a CANONIC EPISODE à 2 (Subj. and Answer)

Subject _____   Subject _____

Answer _____   Answer

Subject _____   Subject _____

Answer _____   Answer

88   89   90   91

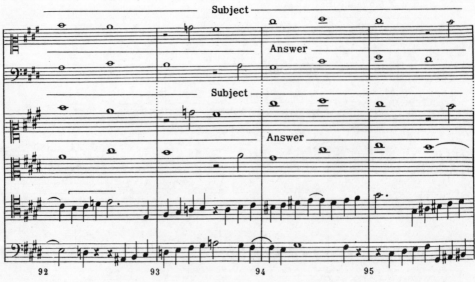

_____ Subject _____

Answer _____

Subject _____

Answer _____

92   93   94   95

6th STRETTO (canon à 4)
over a tonic pedal

rall.

Largo

290

Fugue in 4 Voices

(Institute Competition, 1883)

Subject by Massenet

Paul VIDAL[1]
Class of Massenet

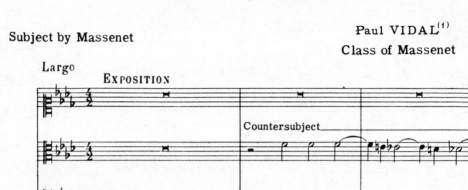

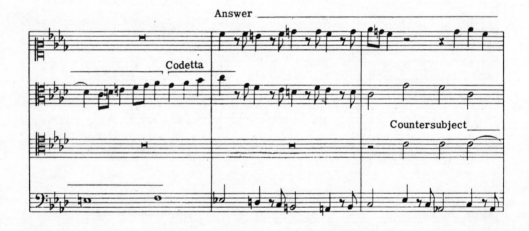

1. First Grand Prix de Rome, 1883

Countersubject _____ EPISODE

based on the countersubject

Dominant pedal

296

STRETTO

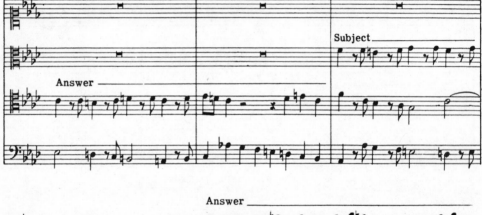

4th STRETTO in inversion

Pedal on the tonic

Subject

dimin.

Fugue in 4 Voices

Subject by A. Gedalge

Ch. KŒCHLIN
Classes of Massenet
and G. Fauré

EPISODE based on the Ad lib. part, A and on frags. of the Subject

Dominant pedal

Canon of the subject & the answer

3rd STRETTO

Fugue in 4 Voices

(Preliminary Competition, 1896)

Subject by A. Gedalge

Florent. Schmitt[1]
Classes of Massenet and G. Fauré

1. First Grand Prix de Rome, 1900

310

Dominant pedal

312

Fugue in 4 Voices

Subject by A. Gedalge

Mlle. J. Boulay[1]
Class of Massenet

EXPOSITION

1. First Prize for Fugue, 1897

316

KEY OF THE 2nd DEGREE

Countersubject

Subject

KEY OF THE 4th DEGREE
Subject

C.S.

EPISODE based on the end of the subject

320

321

Fugue in 4 Voices

(with three countersubjects)

Subject by Georges Enesco

Georges Enesco
Class of Massenet

KEY OF THE 3rd DEGREE

EPISODE based on C.S. 3 and a fragment of the subject

KEY OF THE 6th DEGREE

326

FUGUE SUBJECTS

□ □ □

A.

For the Study of the Exposition

1) A. GEDALGE

2) A. GEDALGE

3) A. GEDALGE

4) Anon.

5) Anon.

6) A. THOMAS

7) A. THOMAS

8) A. THOMAS

9) GEVAERT

10) RADEGLIA

11) GOUNOD

328

12) A.THOMAS

13) GUILMANT

14) Anon.

15) REBER

16) MASSENET

17) SAINT-SAËNS

B.

For the Study of the Stretto

18) A.GEDALGE

19) A.GEDALGE

20) A.GEDALGE

21) MATHESON

22) A.GEDALGE

23) A.GEDALGE

24) BATTIFFERRI

25) J.S.BACH

C.

Miscellaneous Subjects

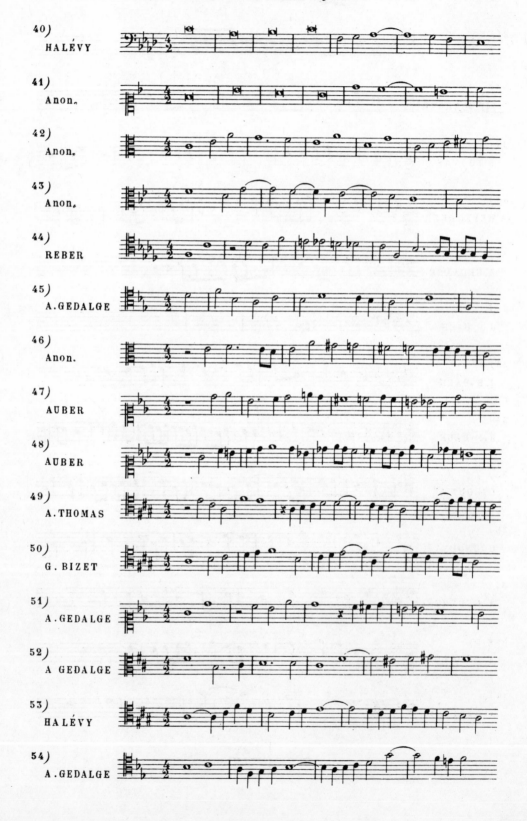

332

333

336

337

338

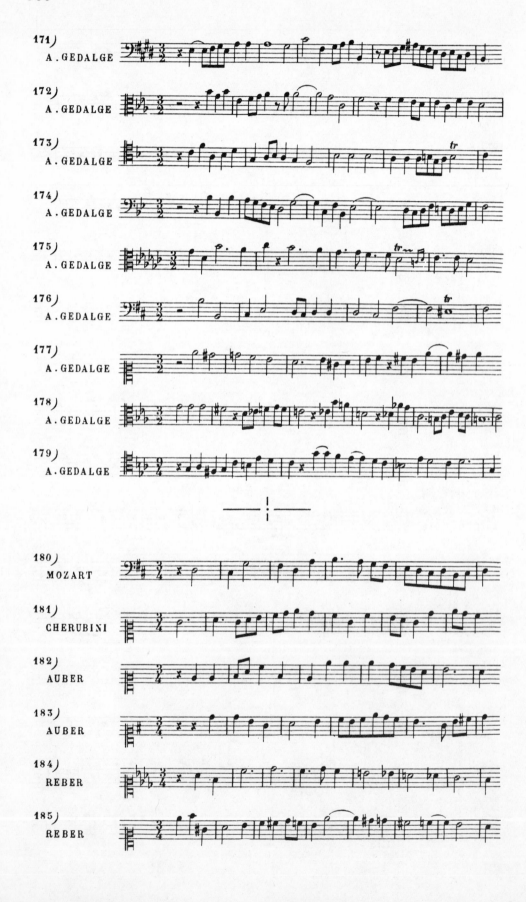

Index

(the numbers refer to sections, not to pages)

use of two countersubjects, 106, 113, 114

use of two countersubjects in the exposition, 150, 151, 152; examples, 174, 175

never written on the answer, but always on the subject, 111

Degrees

first degree: beginning a subject, 39, 40, 41, 59; ending a subject, 40, 41; as the root of the tonic triad, 35

second degree: beginning a subject, 103

third degree (mediant): beginning a subject, 37, 39, 40; ending a subject, 40, 41; as the third of the tonic chord, 36

fourth degree: altered, keeps its character as leading tone of the dominant key, 45, 102; beginning a subject, 103; unaltered, considered as seventh degree of the dominant, 63, 69, 70

fifth degree: beginning a subject, 37, 42; ending a subject, 85; as the first degree of the dominant key, 37; its tonal role, 52, 53, 55, 56, 57, 58

sixth degree: beginning a subject, 103

seventh degree of the major mode, or unaltered in the minor mode: cannot begin a subject in the minor mode, 101; its harmonic and tonal function, 60, 64; in a subject beginning on the tonic and going directly to the seventh degree, 59, 60, 62, 64, 66, 100

seventh degree of the minor mode, altered: beginning a subject, is considered as leading tone of the main key, 101; as leading tone of the main key when it follows the tonic and is followed immediately by the dominant, 61; as third of the tonic triad of the dominant key, 64, 65

tonal determination of, coming between the tonic (or mediant) occurring as the first note of the subject and the dominant, 62, 63, 64, 65, 66

Development

of the fugue, 397, 398

of a musical idea, 396, 397, 398

(see also Episode)

Diminution

double, 254

in the episode, 252

with inversion, retrograde, retrograde inversion, 253

in the stretto, 304, 305, 306, 307, 308; against original time-values, 306, 307, 308

of the subject, 195, 201

Entries

of the answer in the exposition, 133; 138, 140, 141

of the countersubject: after a codetta, 134; after the first entry of the subject (with the answer) 128, 132

on a figure taken from the subject, countersubject, or free parts of the exposition, 257

how to make them, 499

their number: in the exposition, 226; in the stretto, 261, 359, 360

preceded by a rest, 145, 256, 499

of the subject: after a cadence, 406; at a perfect cadence, 402, 407, 408, 409

successive, of several countersubjects, 128, 129, 130

two, in succession, of subject and answer, must not be in the same order of parts, 499

Episode

with augmentation, examples, 251

with augmentation and diminution in inversion, example, 253

canonic, 234; examples, 234, 235; construction of, 236 237: examples, 238, 239

combinations possible (six) 215

a) each part imitates itself, using a figure distinct from the others, 216; examples from Bach, 226

b) all the parts are derived from the main motive, which remains in one of the parts, 217: examples from Bach, 218, 219, 220, 221, 222, 224

c) two parts imitate each other, the others imitate themselves, 225; examples, 225, 226

d) the parts imitate each other two by two, 227; examples of Mozart, Bach, 227

e) three parts imitate each other, 228; examples from Bach, 228, 229, 230

f) all the parts imitate each other, 231; examples from Bach, 231, 233, from Handel, 232

constructed on several combinations,

possible, 14

head of, 21

imitative treatment and at least one close canon with the answer must be possible, 13

length, 15, 16, 17

melody, 12

a melodic phrase which is complete in its musical sense, 9

modality: it belongs entirely to one mode, 18

modulates to the dominant key: when it begins on the dominant, 37, 42; when, beginning with the tonic or mediant, it goes directly to the fifth degree, 37, 59, or to the seventh degree (unaltered in the minor mode) followed by the fifth degree, 59; if it has or implies an alteration characteristic of the dominant key, 44, 77; if it ends with the dominant or the seventh degree unaltered in the minor mode) 85, examples analyzed, 86, 87, 88

does not modulate: when it begins and ends with the tonic or mediant without touching the fifth degree, 39; when, beginning and ending on the tonic or mediant, it does not go immediately to the fifth degree or to the seventh degree followed by the fifth, but touches the dominant as a passing tone, an auxiliary tone, or in a sequence, 40, examples analyzed, 40, 41

modulation by an alteration characteristic of the dominant key, 33, 74, 77

after a modulation on the initial note, it must return to the main key, 43, 74

modulations peculiar to the head and end of, 34

range of its melody, 12

its rhythm, 11

tonal interpretations of, 78; examples analyzed, 79, 80, 81, 82, 83, 84

tonality: limited to the keys of the first and fifth degrees, 19, 20; must, for the most part, be in the key of its first degree, 43

Supplementary parts

in the conclusion of the fugue, 382

with the pedal, 330, 382

Theme of the fugue (see Subject, Answer, Episode, Modulation)

Unison

avoided between the last note of the subject and the first note of the answer, 137

avoided between entries in the stretto, 269

Unity

of expression in a fugue, 415, 421, 423

melodic, in a fugue, 422, 423, 424, 425

of style in a fugue, 415